Freedom From Your Past

Jimmy Evans
& Ann Billington

**A Christian Guide to
Personal Healing and
Restoration**

MarriageToday™
PO Box 59888
Dallas, Texas 75229
972-953-0500
www.marriagetoday.com

All examples in this book involving ministry situations are real. However, the details and surrounding circumstances may have been altered or combined to preserve the privacy and confidentiality of the individuals involved.

For simplicity, the masculine pronoun is used when referring to people in general terms; it is intended to be interchangeable with the feminine.

Cover design by Chris Hendrixson.

Scripture quotations are taken from the *New American Standard Bible* (NASB), copyright© 1960, 1962, 1963, 1968, 1971, 1972, 1973, 1975, 1977 by The Lockman Foundation, LaHabre, California. Scriptures noted *New King James Version* (NKJV), copyright© 1979, 1980, 1982, Thomas Nelson, Inc., Publishers; or *King James Version* (KJV).

Library of Congress Catalog Card Number: 95-80154

ISBN 978-1-931585-05-9

14 13 12 11 10 9 8 7 6

Printed in the United States of America.

Acknowledgments

To Jesus, Who set me free from my past and has given me a new and wonderful life. I continue to be overwhelmed by His love, mercy, and grace.

To my loving wife, Karen, whose prayers, patience, and partnership through the years have been an inspiration and strength through good times and bad.

So many people are involved in the publication of a book like this. I have a wonderful staff of dedicated people who press toward the goal of the high calling of Christ. Their dedication and professionalism make me proud of them.

To the board of directors, the elders of Trinity Fellowship Church, and the many friends who have stood by Karen and me all of these years—thank you. Words can't express how much we love and appreciate you.

Ann Billington, 1947-2000

Ann Billington went to be with the Lord in the winter of 2000. Ann had a zest for life and a burning passion to see people delivered and set free from the issues that encumbered them. Her effectiveness as a counselor and teacher continues to bear fruit to this day and those she ministered to will forever appreciate the wisdom, spiritual truth, and discernment that enabled her to be a vessel of healing for God to pour through.

Contents

Introduction

"Lie down on the couch and tell me about your childhood." Those are the classic words many of us think when we imagine a psychiatrist beginning the process of trying to help a patient. But is it really necessary—not lying down on the couch or seeing a psychiatrist, but bringing up our childhood and the issues of our past? Isn't there another way to deal with our problems? Do Christians have to use the same techniques as the rest of the world to get solutions to their problems? All of those are important questions to consider.

First, let me deal with the question of bringing up the past in order to deal with some of the present issues in our lives. I don't believe that you need to dredge up every event in your life in order to get the help and healing you may need. In fact, feeling a need to dismantle every previous event in your life can lead to as great a bondage as many of the problems you may currently face.

Even though we don't need to hyper-scrutinize our past, we do need to understand the association between our lives today and some of the more significant events in our past. Without a doubt, the two are inseparably linked. The entire premise of this book is based upon this statement: The past is not the past until it has been reconciled in Christ. Another way to make that statement is this: The significant events, people, and issues of our past which caused us personal pain or problems are still negatively affecting our lives today unless we have dealt with them properly.

We need to understand that our parents, siblings, peers, heritage, society, experiences, and personal decisions all have a powerful and lasting effect upon our lives. It's simply not possible to disconnect ourselves completely from those people and things which comprise our past just by virtue of our salvation or the years between us and an event. In other words, they can still be affecting our attitudes, behaviors, personalities, fears, relational ability, health, or view of the world and of God.

When this is understood, it isn't necessary to go on a subliminal journey through our memories or get mad and blame our problems on the world. We simply need to take an inventory of those significant events in our lives which have affected us and learn how to deal with them so they become past issues which have no negative influence on our lives today. In many cases, it may be a simple but important process which frees us from certain emotions or obstacles. In other cases, it may be a more painful process because of a deeper hurt or problem from our past. However, the deeper the hurt, the greater become the problems that are caused in our lives today. But even more important—the greater is the freedom that will take place when we reconcile those issues of our past.

Another significant issue which needs to be addressed is the issue of the "secular" versus "Christian" approach to getting help. For some people, reviewing the past and dealing with it constitutes a pagan practice. Many of these people stand upon the premise that all of our past hurts and problems are to be buried at the cross when we get saved, and we are simply to leave them there. According to these people, if one has any problems, one simply nails them to the cross or endures them for the glory of God and proceeds forth.

Even though there are many issues which need to die at the cross and others we may have to endure for a season, or even for the rest of our lives, it is extremely wrong for anyone to believe that dealing with our past is a "secular" or "worldly" practice. What we must realize is this: Jesus didn't die on the cross to give us the ability to deny or ignore our problems. He died on the cross so we could deal with them and overcome them. Because of Jesus' victory on the cross and the power of His resurrection life, we are enabled to look squarely at any event, past or present, and to thoroughly and victoriously deal with it. Being unable or unwilling to do this isn't a virtuous Christian act—it is an ignorant, unfortunate one.

Today, many Christians suffer needlessly because they either don't know how to reconcile their past or someone has told them they shouldn't. We see these people every day in counseling. Our desire for them is that they become able to function in their relationships and pursuits in life in a healthy, positive way. We also want to see them free in the Lord to be able to seek and serve Him with zeal and desire. We don't want them to stare

> *Jesus didn't die on the cross to give us the ability to deny or ignore our problems. He died on the cross so we could deal with them and overcome them.*

constantly backward or mysteriously inward "for the glory of God." We want them to be able to simply and succinctly deal with the issues of their past in a totally biblical, Spirit-led manner and then to be able to move forever forward, with their past as a reconciled issue and not as an invisible tether of pain and needless limitations.

> *This book will give you the tools and skills necessary to be able to reconcile your past in Christ and go forward to accomplish God's will for your life.*

In response to this, some might still say, "Well, the Apostle Paul said that he had forgotten what was in his past and pressed forward toward the mark, and that's what we need to do. Just forget the past and go on!" What I would say in response and what this book will say to you is this: The Apostle Paul was able to forget the past, not because of his desire to be an emotional martyr or his ability to erase his memory. Rather, he could forget his past because it was reconciled in Christ. The people who had harmed him had been forgiven; the events of his upbringing were dealt with, and every other significant thing in his past had been successfully resolved by the power that only Jesus Christ can give.

This book will give you the tools and skills necessary to be able to reconcile your past in Christ and go forward to accomplish God's will for your life. It has been our prayer and concerted task within the pages of this book to be totally biblical and painstakingly balanced in all that we say. We realize that only the truth of God will set us free. Our encouragement comes from the fact that we, as well as hundreds of others to whom we have ministered, have been set free by these truths. We hope you will be another one touched by God, as you face your past and become forever free to experience a wonderful future.

Jimmy Evans
Dallas, Texas

Section I

Freedom From Your Past

Preparing for Freedom

The Secret of Your Freedom

Chapter 1 Ann Billington

It seemed so easy, so quick, so painless. In minutes it would be over. I would close my eyes, go to sleep and, unlike Sleeping Beauty, never awaken again. My life at twenty-five didn't read like a fairy tale. Instead, it was more of a tragedy fraught with pain, disappointment, and failure. I couldn't foresee any happy ever after, only darkness and dread. If you had known me then, you would have never guessed the misery that lay just beneath the professional, capable facade I presented to the world. No one would have dreamed I was sitting on the bathroom cabinet, holding forty Darvon capsules, contemplating suicide.

As I considered my death, a voice seemingly from nowhere penetrated my consciousness. It said, "There is a better way." At the same time I could instantly see in my mind a picture of three books, two black ones and a large orange one. I had seen them the week before in a department store. With this mental picture capturing my thoughts, I put the capsules back in the bottle, capped it, and went to bed.

> Never would I have to fear the punishment and torment of hell I could sleep at night. confident that at my death I would be taken into the presence of Jesus.

The next morning, I greeted the store manager as he unlocked the doors. Going directly to the book section, I located the three books. The orange book was *The New American Standard Bible*. It surprised me to discover that the Bible came in a version other than the King James. Upon returning home with my purchase, I opened the Bible for the first time in approximately fifteen years. Having been raised in church, I was familiar with religion, but as I was soon to learn, religion and Jesus were not necessarily the same thing. Even though I had rejected most of what I had learned in childhood about God, as I opened my new Bible I was determined to believe what I read. Soon thereafter my eyes fell upon a Scripture passage in Matthew 11:28-30 which reads, *"Come to Me, all you who labor and are heavy laden, and I will give you rest. Take My yoke upon you and learn from Me, for I am gentle and lowly in heart, and you will find rest for your souls. For My yoke is easy and My burden is light."*

The instant I finished reading that passage, I made the decision to give my burden to God and to take His "yoke." That decision completely changed my life and my eternal destination. My life has never been the same since. Instantly,

God accomplished two goals in me: one for the future and one for the present. First, my final and eternal address was secured. Heaven was my eternal home. Never would I have to fear the punishment and torment of hell. I could sleep at night, confident that at my death I would be taken into the presence of Jesus. For most of us that would be enough, but Jesus offers more.

The second objective accomplished that day was the opportunity for an intimate relationship with God through His Son Jesus. As believers, we have the privilege to know God in a personal way. Sadly, many Christians don't understand this is possible here on earth before we die. Instead, we reserve "real" relationships for our human counterparts, not realizing we can have a dynamic, fulfilling, loving relationship with Jesus Christ. With this false assumption, man is forced to accept a brittle, empty shell of religion, learning to survive the best way he can until he dies or until Jesus comes again. However, this wasn't God's original plan.

God's primary goal from the beginning was relationship. Adam and Eve were created with the ability to relate to God and each other in an intimate way. Separation from God was never His intention; it was the result of man's sin. Therefore, since the time of the fall of man, God has endeavored to restore His relationship with us. Now that the redemptive work of the cross is finished, man can be restored into an intimate relationship with God. This personal relationship with God is the secret of gaining true freedom. Only in a personal relationship with God can we find the healing and fulfillment of our souls that will truly set us free.

However, in order to have the intimacy with God He desires for us, we must first accept the fact that God is a relational being capable of an intimate relationship with us. God is a "person" and as such has the inherent ability to relate on the deepest level. The Bible is full of accounts of God trying to reveal Himself to man in a very personal manner. In Exodus 33:13 Moses boldly entreats God to "... *show me now Your way, that I may know You.*" God responds in verse eighteen of that chapter by showing Moses His glory. This passage of Scripture reveals something about the personality of God. He desires to reveal Himself to man. In fact, the name *Jehovah* in the Old Testament means, "The self-existent One who reveals Himself."

Paul also revealed a desire to know God intimately in Philippians 3:8 when he said: "*Yet indeed I also count all things loss for the excellence of the knowledge of Christ Jesus my Lord, for whom I have suffered the loss of all things, and count them as rubbish, that I may gain Christ*" (NKJV). Again in Philippians 3:10, Paul reveals his desire to know Christ: "*... that I may know Him and the power of His resurrection, and the fellowship of His sufferings, being conformed to His death*" (NKJV).

Nothing in Paul's life was more important than his relationship with Christ—not his Jewish pedigree, his social status, or his Roman citizenship. His primary goal and purpose was to know Jesus. Shouldn't this be the cry in the heart of every Christian—to know God?

A friend's husband was in the military and stationed in Turkey. They were separated for a year and were unable to communicate except by mail and infrequently by phone. They became so hungry to hear each other's voice that they resorted to cassette tapes instead of letters. Few marriages would flourish if they were forced to communicate by long distance for such an extended period. Yet we settle for a similar relationship with God—speaking to Him as though He were far away and not expecting a personal answer.

When Jesus died, the veil between the Holy Place and the Holy of Holies in the Temple was split open, forever abolishing the barrier between God and man. Hebrews 10:19-22 expresses it this way: *"Therefore, brethren, having boldness to enter the Holiest by the blood of Jesus, by a new and living way which He consecrated for us, through the veil, that is, His flesh and having a High Priest over the house of God, let us draw near with a true heart in full assurance of faith, having our hearts sprinkled from an evil conscience and our bodies washed with pure water"* (NKJV).

Through His blood shed for our sins, Jesus bought us entry into the very presence of God. Relationship is possible with a holy God. So, knowing relationship with God is achievable while on earth, what blocks our entry into His presence? Why does it appear that people are going through the religious motions without joy and peace? Why do we fail to take advantage of such an incredible offer?

Sin is the obvious first answer. The wages of sin is death, and sin separates us from God. When we know there is unrepentant sin in our lives or we are just simply aware of how imperfect we are, we tend to stay away from God. However, I propose that sin is not the average Christian's greatest obstacle in relating to God.

The greatest problem most of us have in relating intimately to God lies in the unhealed and unresolved issues of our past, which twist our understanding and perceptions of God. Each of us was raised in a less than perfect environment, and that environment has left its imprint on our lives, which in turn affects our relationship with God. For example, my father was a distant and non-relational individual who was detached from the family. However, he was a good man and a good provider. Though he cared that we were nurtured, he didn't involve himself in that process. Consequently, I tended to view God in the same light. He was a good God who saw to my needs, but stayed detached from me personally.

Perhaps you were neglected or abused by your father. That event alone would color your concepts of trust, authority, and love. Unfortunately, we almost always transfer those concepts to God. The result is a relationship that remains shallow and unfulfilling while God earnestly desires a close, personal relationship with us. How then are these issues resolved?

Most of us have learned to cope to some degree with troublesome problems from our past. But coping is not enough. Jesus wants to heal you. To cope means you learn to tolerate existing situations. Healing means the removal of those issues. Isaiah 61:1-3 says: *"The Spirit of the Lord GOD is upon Me, because the LORD has anointed Me to preach good tidings to the poor; He has sent Me to heal the brokenhearted, to proclaim liberty to the captives, and the opening of the prison to those who are bound; to proclaim the acceptable year of the LORD, and the day of vengeance of our God; to comfort all who mourn, to console those who mourn in Zion, to give them beauty for ashes, the oil of joy for mourning, the garment of praise for the spirit of heaviness; that they may be called trees of righteousness, the planting of the LORD, that He may be glorified"* (NKJV).

Jesus doesn't promise to help us cope. He promises freedom and healing that will enable us to move into a fulfilling relationship with Him and others. Consequently, Jesus will not rest until He has healed us and drawn us to Himself. So, as God snatched me from an eternity in hell, He simultaneously began a healing process that would enable me to know and relate to Him.

Therefore, if God desires to heal us and reconcile us to Himself, it stands to reason that He has provided the answers necessary to accomplish that goal in us. These answers are found in the Bible. Every solution to every problem mankind encounters can be found in the Bible. The book of Genesis reveals that man is a triune being, composed of body, mind, and spirit. God created Adam out of the dust of the ground with an intellect sufficient to take dominion over the earth. He then breathed into him the breath of life, giving Adam a spirit that could commune with God.

Though Adam catapulted humanity into a fallen state, thanks to the cross, redeemed man can relate to God on three levels: body, mind, and spirit. Too often, however, man fails to recognize the spiritual dimensions of his life. He assumes that he is restricted to what he perceives with his mind and body, negating the relevancy of the spirit. To be effective, healing must take place on all three levels of existence.

As I sat on that bathroom cabinet, it was clear from my behavior that I had many problems. Had I taken my problems to an individual who didn't believe in the spiritual realm, he would have attempted to change only observable behavior. That type of help gives a certain level of comfort. However, it's not enough. Man is a spiritual being and must approach his problems from the spiritual level as well.

Healing the mind, body, and spirit is similar to nurturing a tree. A tree is made of three basic parts—the roots, the sap, and the body. In caring for a tree, it is important to prune off dead branches. Yearly, it becomes necessary to spray for insects, bores, or fungus. To attend to the needs of that tree based on what lies above ground is definitely important.

> *Though Adam catapulted humanity into a fallen state, thanks to the cross, redeemed man can relate to God on three levels: body, mind, and spirit.*

However, there is more. Underneath is a complex root system that sustains, nourishes, and supports the tree. The root system must be nourished as well. Without it, no amount of pruning, spraying, or medicating will completely restore a sick tree to health. God approaches healing in much the same way.

When we have problems and sins in our lives, we many times deal with them like the person trying to heal a tree while ignoring the root system. Since pleasing God is important, we begin to prune our branches. We saw, we trim, we medicate, all in an effort to cut away bad habits and sin. Though this can accomplish a certain level of change, it won't bring total victory. Man cannot effectively change his behavior without also changing his heart. Man's heart cannot be changed except by the Spirit. The unseen root system must also be treated. To address behavior, thought life, and feeling without attending to the root issues of the heart won't bring total victory.

> Man cannot effectively change his behavior without also changing his heart.

Though suicide and depression were obvious manifestations of my problems, attention to those areas alone never would have achieved healing. A subterranean root system comprised of iniquities, demonic activity, unforgiveness, judgments, and inner vows ran beneath the surface of my life. From that root system, a host of outward manifestations began to bear fruit in my life. That fruit may take the form of suicide as it did in me, or perhaps addictions, anger, or sinful performance. Regardless, the roots must be dealt with to produce healthy fruit, and healthy fruit is evidenced in healthy relationships with man and God.

With all the self-help books available on the market today, it is tempting to put Jesus in a box. We think if we can find just the right formula, we can find happiness and healing. However, my own experience is that Jesus is too big for any box, and every time you think you have found the formula for healing, it changes. Even though there are many helpful principles to help us toward freedom, they are all incomplete unless they lead us to a personal relationship with Christ. Even though His truth is eternal, He ministers that truth to us by His Spirit in a personal, intimate way. He knows exactly where we are and every past event of our lives. Through relationship, not formulas, He will heal us and set us free from our past.

When our daughter was young, she frequently came downstairs holding in her tiny hands a knotted, twisted nest of silver chains and necklaces—the sum total of all the jewelry she owned. She held up her hands to her daddy, asking him to "Fix it, please." He reached down, took the jewelry from her hands and placing it on the cabinet, began to painstakingly unravel the twisted mass. Ever so gently he unknotted the chains, untangled the strands, and freeing them from their prison, laid each piece straight and whole on the counter.

Our lives are similar to those chains. We, too, come to our heavenly Father holding the twisted, knotted tangle of our lives, and lifting our hands up to God, we ask Him to "Fix it, please." He reaches down and takes our knotted, hurting hearts, and though He now has our hearts, He does not stop there. He lays our lives out in front of Him and begins the process of untangling the issues and hurts that have besieged us for so long. Ever so gently and carefully, He frees us from our prison of pain and conflict, laying to rest each issue of our lives, straight, untangled, and unknotted. Why does He do this for us? Because He loves us and wants to enjoy us and allow us to enjoy Him and each other. Personal, passionate, pure love is His motivation toward you right now and for the rest of your life.

As you proceed prayerfully through this book, God will begin a process that will untangle the problem issues of your life. Allow God to reveal the roots and fruits of your life that have hindered your relationship with Him and others. The secret of your freedom is in opening your heart to God, and through a personal encounter with Him, experiencing the power of His healing love only His presence can bring.

Before continuing in the book, consider praying this prayer or one similar to it. It will prepare you for His healing and blessing as you gain freedom from your past and renewed hope and vision for your future: *"Father, in the Name of Jesus I open my heart to you. I confess that I am a sinner and have sinned against You and others. I receive the death and resurrection of Jesus Christ and the power of His blood as the payment for my sins. By faith, I receive Your forgiveness. Also, by faith I receive You into my heart. Thank You for loving me in spite of my sins and failures. Thank You for your wonderful grace that receives back a prodigal son and restores him to the relationship he left in sin. I commit myself to You and the process of healing and restoration in my life. Fill me with your Holy Spirit and change me until I am whole, healthy, and in right relationship with You and those You have placed in my life. Please bless me and lead me. In Jesus' Name, Amen!"*

The School of Freedom

Chapter 2 Jimmy Evans

The journey to freedom is a wonderful journey. Though it means change and some unexpected turns, the destination of freedom is worth everything we give for it. And once you're free, it's hard to believe you ever lived any other way. That is the way I feel about life today.

For years of my adult Christian life, I lived in different types of bondage. Some of the bondages were emotional, some mental, some spiritual, and some were even physical or of my flesh. The bondages of my life affected my outlook on life and my future. They affected my relationships with everyone around me, especially those who were close to me. They affected my ability to understand God and, to some degree, even my desire to seek Him. Bondage, despite the nature or the source, has a significant effect on our lives and the lives of those around us.

In becoming free from many of these bondages, I learned a lot about the process of healing and becoming free. Even though I'm grateful for the outcome of the ministry and teaching I received that produced the healing in my life, I wish someone had given me more information concerning the process of becoming free and what to expect. If they had, it would have made a lot of the process easier to accept and understand.

As you proceed toward receiving some healing and freedom through this book, this chapter will explain to you three truths you will need to understand and accept if you are going to be set free. In understanding these things now, it will help you immeasurably as you are faced with opportunities to be set free later in this book as well as later in life.

Using the metaphor of the "School of Freedom" as the backdrop, the remainder of this chapter will introduce you to the three classrooms. To become truly free, you must visit and graduate successfully from each of these classrooms. Each is unique, and anyone can graduate successfully. However, they all have one thing in common—they are each indispensable elements in finding the freedom we need and God wants us to have.

The Classroom of Reality

One of the first things we must understand in order to be healed and set free is this: Only the truth has the power to make us truly free (John 8:32). You would think that in addressing Christian people this would be a rather easy point to sell. However, even though Christians give lip service to their faith in the power of truth, to many of us, it never translates into reality.

The first classroom we must succeed in is the classroom where what we think and believe, or what we don't want to think or believe, all submits itself to the truth. For this to happen, we must accept two realities.

Reality 1: Our perception of reality may be wrong.

A false reality builds itself around the stronghold of pride. This is why Jesus couldn't minister freedom to the arrogant and deceived Pharisees. They had a number of bondages that needed to be broken and which had been passed on for numerous generations. However, they refused their healing because they rejected the truth of Jesus.

Could you be wrong—wrong about people, about the judgments you've made throughout life, about how you've dealt with your hurts and problems, or maybe even about how you haven't dealt with them? When you come to the point of admitting the fact that you could be wrong and need Jesus to minister His truth to you, you are then at a point of receiving freedom.

Reality 2: Only God has the truth.

Jesus stated plainly to His disciples in John 14:6, *"I am the way, the truth and the life. No one comes to the Father but through Me."* Jesus uses the definite article *the* in relation to Himself being truth. He didn't say He was *a* truth. He said He was *the* truth.

The classroom of reality will permit only one teacher, Jesus, to speak. Every other voice must submit to His voice, and every other source of so-called "truth" must bow its knee to Him. He won't compete with other religions, watered down "gospels," current-day psychological gurus, or what you think or feel.

A person who wants to argue with Jesus is put out of the class. The only people permitted in the classroom are those who have accepted His Lordship and are willing to seek and submit to what He teaches. The Bible is the exalted source of learning in Jesus' classroom of reality. It is honored as an infallible and inspired source by those who progress and graduate. It is also held far above all other sources of information by those who have found reality.

> *Those who will receive His truth are set free; those who won't—aren't.*

If you're not sure the Bible is true or you believe that competing voices in the world may have a better answer than Jesus, you're not ready for the classroom of reality. I found out a long time ago that Jesus won't apologize for what He has to say, nor will He argue with unbelievers or believers who doubt His Word. He speaks clearly by His Word and through His Spirit the truth we need to hear. The Spirit and the Word are always in total agreement. Those who will receive His truth are set free; those who won't—aren't.

Before going on, I want to make one other point regarding reality. For many people who are in bondage, their problem isn't just deception; it's denial. One of the most common ways people deal with pain and problems is to deny them—to pretend they don't hurt, they didn't happen, or that everything is okay when it's not. The curse of denial is that it ensures perpetual bondage. As I heard it said once, "The cornerstone of bondage is denial." The opposite is "The cornerstone of freedom is truth." The classroom of reality demands a truthful answer to every question. Our Teacher, Jesus, knows when we are lying. And He responds the same way to denial as He does to deception because both are different forms of dishonesty and error.

Freedom from our past cannot be gained by playing games or giving the answers we wish were true. Likewise, even if something has been buried in the basement of our hearts for years through denial, its dead carcass produces a stench for every other room of our lives. You can try "air freshener" or other superficial means as you probably have already done, but the truth remains: Real freedom will only be experienced as you peel back the doors of pain and pretense to let the light of God remove the carcass of the past which needs to go.

Remember this: The price of allowing the truth into your life is temporary discomfort followed by a lifetime of freedom and joy. The price of deception or denial is temporary sedation from the distasteful and painful issues we want to avoid, followed by a lifetime of emotional, spiritual, and relational problems. The price to pay is the price of truth. When you pay the price, you are ready to proceed to the next classroom.

The Classroom of Responsibility

One of the more common ways people deal with their problems is to make someone else responsible. The classic case of this problem is those people who remain emotionally unhealed throughout their lives as they blame their parents and/or someone else for their inadequacies. All of us know someone like this. Even though they are precious, these people are filled with anger and are paralyzed to some degree in life by an invisible umbilical cord constantly feeding their todays from the haunting memories of their dark yesterdays. The results are self-pity, fear, negative attitudes, and hopelessness concerning the future.

We must understand the extreme danger of making someone else responsible for our problems. The danger focuses on this false assumption: If someone else is responsible for my problems, then that person is also responsible for the solution to my problems. Therefore, my obedience or action won't help my situation; *he or she* must act. This very mindset is what keeps many people in bondage. They are forever waiting for someone else to change, apologize, or make everything all right. Most people who wait for this response are disappointed at best. Many waste an entire lifetime expecting someone else to solve a problem they could and should have taken responsibility for long ago.

One of the critical truths we must understand in order to gain the freedom we need is this: Our experiences in life don't have complete control over our destiny—our responses to life's events are also a factor. It's not our parents, siblings, peers, or teachers who are primarily responsible for our happiness and health; it's us! Even though other people have a responsibility before God for how they treat us, we are ultimately responsible for our behavior.

As a pastor, I've heard the stories of thousands of people through the years concerning abuse, abandonment, disappointment, and disasters in their childhoods and past lives. What is interesting to me is the wide variety of responses to these situations. For many people who come from terrible backgrounds, they live happily and successfully today because they decided to respond to their problems in a positive, godly manner. They took responsibility to forgive, turn to God, and go on with their lives.

I've seen many others with essentially the same problems constantly licking their wounds, blaming their families, and refusing to face life today. The common denominator in these people is their refusal to take responsibility and to do what is right. They have transferred that responsibility to someone else. So they live their lives in a poisonous fixation upon their abuse and abusers, yielding their futures to the idol of irresponsibility.

One illustration of the extreme danger of refusing to take responsibility for ourselves comes from the biblical story of

Cain and Abel who were both bringing an offering to God. The implication of the text is that God had commanded Cain and Abel to bring Him an acceptable offering. Acceptability in God's sight was obviously linked with the quality of their offering and whether or not it represented the best they had to give.

Related to Abel's offering, the Bible says this in Genesis 4:4: *"Abel also brought of the firstborn of his flock and of their fat. And the Lord respected Abel and his offering ..."* (NKJV). The real significance of God's "respect" for Abel's offering was in the fact that Abel gave his best. He took the responsibility to do what God instructed, so the end result was God's blessing and approval.

Concerning Cain's offering to the Lord, Genesis 4:3 simply records that Cain brought "an offering." Nothing of the quality or quantity of Cain's offering is recorded because there wasn't anything special about it. It wasn't his best or what God had instructed him to bring. It was simply "an offering" that was convenient. No doubt, he rationalized his poor performance. However, regardless of what was going on in Cain's mind when he brought the offering, God was clearly not pleased.

Genesis 4:5 records God's response to Cain and his offering: *"... He did not respect Cain and his offering ..."* In response to God's lack of blessing for his offering, the verse continues, *"And Cain was very angry, and his countenance fell."* Rather than realizing his own disobedience and irresponsibility, Cain blamed God. He was angry at God and his brother Abel because things didn't go well for him.

After seeing Cain's response to His lack of respect for his offering, God spoke these words to Cain: *"If you do well, will you not be accepted? And if you do not do well sin lies at the door. And its desire is for you, but you should rule over it"* (Genesis 4:7, NKJV). These are powerful words that come from God, not only to Cain, but to all of us. God makes three simple but powerful points in His words to Cain that we all must recognize and understand:

1. We are responsible for our own behavior.
2. Our obedience or lack of obedience to every situation leads to happiness or unhappiness.
3. Satan preys upon the irresponsible.

Cain's response to God's words was impudent and arrogant. As soon as God had admonished him, Cain was in his brother's face. Evidently, Abel was unwilling to take up his brother's offense against God and console him in his sin. As a result, Cain decided to kill his brother. This is the common thinking pattern of the irresponsible: "Make someone else the problem and then attack!"

With Abel's blood freshly spilled, God confronted Cain and asked him where his brother Abel was. Cain's response revealed the classic attitude then and now of those who live their lives in misery: "*Am I my brother's keeper?*" (Genesis 4:9, NKJV). Not only was Cain convinced that he wasn't to be held responsible for his own behavior, but evidently, not for anyone else's either. The hypocrisy in Cain's attitude was that, even though he took no responsibility for his own behavior toward God or his brother, he expected God and his brother to be perfect in their responsibility toward him. All of this illustrates the confusion and hurt which are perpetuated and multiplied the longer we allow irresponsibility to linger within our hearts.

Healing and freedom are built upon the bedrock of this attitude: Regardless of how people treat me or what life does to me, I am responsible for my behavior and attitudes toward God, others and myself. My ultimate responsibility is to God, to do what He commands and to turn to Him for my answers. The person who has this attitude is a person poised for freedom. The people I mentioned earlier in this section, who have the same basic problems as others but who go on to live better lives, are always people who hold this attitude or one close to it.

Stop blaming others for who you are or how you are. Sure, people have hurt you and disappointed you. No doubt, life has thrown you some curves you didn't think you deserved. All of us experience these things; that isn't the question. The question is, "How will you respond?" In order to be healthy and to be set free from the pains and pitfalls of your past, you must hold tightly to the attitude that, no matter what life or people do to you, you will take the responsibility to do what you know is right; and when you don't, you will take the responsibility to repent and turn back to God.

The Classroom of Reconciliation

Webster's Dictionary defines the word *reconcile* this way: "to make friendly again; to settle." In all of our pasts there are certain events we need to "settle" or "make friends with again." These may be simple relational or personal issues we can easily reconcile by forgiving someone or receiving forgiveness

Healing and freedom are built upon the bedrock of this attitude: Regardless of how people treat me or what life does to me, I am responsible for my behavior and attitudes toward God, others and myself.

from God. Hopefully, most of the issues we need to reconcile will be relatively simple to "settle." This book will help you recognize the issues which need to be settled and give you the skills to do so.

You must realize that in learning to reconcile your past, sometimes the process of reconciliation is extremely painful. The tissue boxes in my office have been emptied countless times as I have helped people deal with and reconcile painful issues of their pasts. Even though not every issue is painful, some hurt terribly to think about. As one man said to me when I informed him of his need to talk about the extreme abuse of his past, "I don't know if I can survive retrieving those memories."

People who have very hurtful things in their past often have learned to deny them, bury them, ignore them, make fun of them, or just think about them and get depressed. One thing is true, though, of every person with a painful past—the pain will never go away until you have dealt with it properly. Even though you may think you're doing ok, reality will prove that you're not.

A perfect case in point was the man I spoke of earlier who didn't know if he could survive the retrieval of the memories of his past abuse. Having ignored and denied for years the abuse of his past, he manifested hurt in every area of his life. The overall dysfunction of his life and the threat of losing his family finally drove him to get help. At the core of all his problems was a history of extreme emotional abuse from his father.

I could have counseled this man for months about his personal and marriage problems and never really solved the problem because most of it was the result of deep emotional scars, which had never been healed. All of the relationships in his life were constantly manipulated to cater to the painful areas of his soul. Not only that, he had an eating disorder and a very low self-image that all went back to the problems with his father. Thankfully, this man opened up and dealt with the pain of his past. The result was an immediate initiation of a healing process in his life. Within days, his family reported the changes in his behavior and attitudes. Over a period of months, God restored this man's emotions to a point of health and his life improved dramatically—all of this because he was willing to deal with the hurt of his past.

Like a surgeon who wishes he could cure a terrible disease with simple medication, I wish I could help people overcome terrible pain and scars in their past without talking about them and bringing them into the light, but I can't. Even though painful experiences and memories shouldn't be glorified or prolonged, they do need to be honestly admitted and dealt with. For some of you, this will mean remembering some things that have deep pain attached to them. My heart goes out to you, but please deal with them.

As you pray for the Holy Spirit to lead you and prepare you as you read the remainder of this book, He will be faithful. The valley of the shadow of death is a dreadful place for all of us, but thank God He stays with us. Because of God's promise to always be with us, even in our most difficult moments, we need not fear. Nothing in our past, present, or future is greater than God's love and grace. As you face your past, understand the fact that the Healer will always be at your side—ready to set you free from whatever you are willing to bring to Him.

Let me summarize the essence of what you need to take with you from the "School of Freedom" that will help you greatly as you address the issues of your past. First, freedom demands honesty. Honesty demands humility and dependence upon God. Seek to be completely honest before God and man, and freedom will be yours.

Second, you must take responsibility for your own thoughts and actions. You are not the way you are just because of life's events or other people. Your choices also have had a powerful influence on where you are today. With your heart submitted to God, take responsibility to respond to God and others properly in every event in life.

> You are not the way you are just because of life's events or other people. Your choices also have had a powerful influence on where you are today.

Finally, reconciliation of your past requires settling accounts. For this to happen, you must be willing to face even your darkest memories. In some cases this will mean serious pain. You must make the decision to face temporary pain for the sake of your healing or the result will be a lifetime of pain manifested through different areas of your life and relationships.

Concerning your past, you can run but you cannot hide. Facing your past righteously is the only answer to being able to go on to fulfill your destiny in God. Now that you are a graduate of the "School of Freedom," I pray God's blessings upon you as you seek true and lasting freedom from your past.

Freedom From the Roots of Your Past

Understanding and Breaking the Hidden Ties that Bind You to Your Past

Iniquities: Baggage from the Past

Chapter 3 Jimmy Evans

Craig Leone rose slowly from his table at the local restaurant. He was eating at the same table his father and grandfather had eaten at hundreds of times. As a farmer, Craig worked two sections of land adjacent to his father's property. He was an up-and-coming farmer with a wife, two children, and every man's dream of a future.

As Craig finished his meal and started toward the familiar face of the fifty-five-year-old waitress at the cash register, his eyes caught the bright reflection of a car pulling up in the parking lot. There was nothing really unusual about the car, but there was something extremely unusual about the passengers—they were blacks—coming to a whites-only restaurant.

As Craig handed his meal check and money toward the waitress, his eyes continued to glare toward the five figures moving from the car into the restaurant. Two black adults with their three children standing next to them were barely in the door of the restaurant when Craig made a racial remark to the waitress. In a low tone, she replied with a similar slur as they both smiled briefly and then returned to their previous state.

As Craig passed the couple on the way out the door, he was careful not to make eye contact or give them any indication of his disapproval of their presence in "his" restaurant. He felt justified and even proud of his behavior because he was following what his father and grandfather had taught him all of his life. With the sounds of a lifetime of training in prejudice ringing in his ears, Craig moved deliberately past the couple at the door toward his truck. Once comfortably in, Craig stared angrily at the couple in the restaurant and then uttered a venomous curse.

Even though Craig is completely responsible for his behavior, his father and grandfather also share responsibility with him. You see, Craig's sin of prejudice and hatred toward blacks isn't just his own sin of pride; it is a generational sin which has been passed down from one father and child to the next in his family for hundreds of years.

Before the Civil War, Craig's family owned and traded slaves. During the war, they fought on the Confederate side. After the war, every generation of men in his family up to his grandfather had been members of the Ku Klux Klan. You see, Craig was more than just a racist. He was a preprogrammed, generational racist.

The concept of generational sin was introduced early in the Bible. Adam and Eve's sin has affected every generation of people on this planet. It is called the "fall of man." Even though we weren't in the garden and we didn't commit the sin of eating the forbidden fruit with them, we nevertheless suffer because of their sin.

The same truth applies to our parents. Their behavior, both good and bad, has a profound impact on us. Their attitudes, beliefs about God, methods of discipline, and life values constantly impact our developing souls while we are growing up and, to some degree, even after we are grown. When our parents are righteous, it has an obviously positive impact upon us. However, as in Craig's case, when they are sinful and wrong, the result is an unrighteous influence upon our lives, which normally results in the same sin. Even when we don't follow our parents' sin, our lives are still influenced negatively. The Bible calls this family dynamic "iniquities."

The concept of generational sin or iniquities is first found in Deuteronomy 5:9. Here is what the Lord says to the children of Israel concerning sin and its consequences in subsequent generations. "...for I, the LORD your God, am a jealous God, visiting the iniquity of the fathers upon the children to the third and fourth generations of those who hate Me, but showing mercy to thousands, to those who love Me and keep My commandments" (Deuteronomy 5:9-10, NKJV).

Even though this Scripture specifically addresses the iniquities of fathers upon their children, we need to realize that the issue of iniquities relates to mothers as well. In counseling, we find that the transference of iniquities has little to do with gender and much to do with the influence of both parents. The word *fathers* in Deuteronomy 5:9 can also be translated *ancestors*, thereby including both sexes.

One of the powerful truths of this Scripture relates to the behavior of both parents and how it affects children. God's promise to Moses is the visitation of the iniquities of the parents on their children for up to four generations and the blessing of righteousness to thousands. Even though some might raise an eyebrow at the fact that God would allow children to suffer for parental error, we must also look at the incredible blessing children receive when their parents are righteous. Regardless of which side we see, the truth is that the behavior of parents has a profound impact on their children. We see this truth every day in our society as more children reflect the fallen attitudes and sinful cycles of their apostate parents.

> *I have never met a person, including myself, who didn't have iniquities from his parents to deal with.*

But beyond what is clearly evident in others, each one of us must deal with iniquities in our own lives in order to be free from our past. I have never met a person, including myself, who didn't have iniquities from his parents to deal with. The word *iniquity* in the Hebrew language is derived from the word *avah*, which means, "to bend, twist or distort." An iniquity is a tendency toward a sin or error because of the influence of one's parents and/or family history.

One of the best ways to understand the concept of iniquities is to think about what happens to a tree when it is constantly blown in one direction—it grows with a bend. The same is true of a child who is raised in a home where sin is present—as we all have been. None of our parents is perfect. To the degree our parents are righteous and normal in their behavior is to the same degree we are able to grow up "straight" and healthy. However, when they have attitudes and/or behaviors that are sinful, wrong, or abusive, it creates a direct influence in our lives, which can bend us in a wrong direction.

An example in Scripture of the truth of iniquities comes from the hypocritical Pharisees. As hard-hearted, religious zealots, the hypocrites among the Pharisees were generational persecutors of anything with the life of God in it. They were experts in control, driven by greed, who deceitfully dressed themselves in righteous garments as they preyed upon the weak and vulnerable. Their hypocrisy passed from generation to generation with unadulterated zeal.

The power of their generational iniquities was illustrated in the life of the Apostle Paul. Before his conversion, Paul persecuted the church with a vengeance. Watching the cloaks of those stoning the deacon Stephen, the young Saul stood by, never realizing he opposed the purposes of God. Generations of iniquities and hypocrisy influenced his every thought and action, and like his fathers before him, he was bearing the sin of his fathers one more generation.

Before being delivered up by the Sadducees and hypocritical Pharisees to die on the cross, Jesus reminded them that their fathers and ancestors were the ones who had killed the prophets and men of God before him. Here is what Jesus said to them:

"Woe to you! For you build the tombs of the prophets, and your fathers killed them. In fact, you bear witness that you approve the deeds of your fathers; for they indeed killed them, and you build their tombs. Therefore the wisdom of God also said, 'I will send them prophets and apostles, and some of them they will kill and persecute,' that the blood of all the prophets which was shed from the foundation of the world may be required of this generation, from the blood of Abel to the blood of Zechariah who perished between the altar and the temple. Yes, I say to you, it shall be required of this generation" (Luke 11:47-51, NKJV).

Jesus was aware of the fact that He wasn't just dealing with some men who were against Him; He was dealing with the power of generational sin. This is something we must all understand also. Even though all sin is powerful, there is an even greater power to generational sin. The reason is because it is so deeply entrenched within our lives that it produces a stronger motivation of behavior and requires a special type of dealing to break. Generational sin, unless it is clearly recognized and properly rejected, blinds us to truth and bonds us to the same destructive behavior of those who have gone before us.

An example of the power of generational sin was sitting in my office one day. Jeff and Misti were a couple of twenty-one-year-olds who had been married for three years. They got married because Misti was pregnant. One of the reasons Misti got pregnant in the first place was because she wanted to. Even though Jeff didn't know it at the time, Misti set him up so he would have to marry her and she could get away from her mother's control.

So if she was successful in getting pregnant and getting away from her mother, why was she in my office? She was there because Jeff was ready to leave. After approximately thirty minutes of listening to them, their individual sides of the story, we focused on one of the major reasons for their problems: Misti was a controller.

Beginning with setting Jeff up to get her pregnant, Misti was either in control or trying to get control. Even though Jeff had loved Misti at first, he was now so frustrated with her that it took a great deal of persuasion to keep him from leaving. According to Jeff, he felt stripped of his manhood and constantly manipulated by Misti. As he recounted situation after situation of Misti's control, Misti never denied one of his accusations. Her only defense was that she knew she was wrong and didn't know why she was that way. If Jeff would only stay, she promised she would change.

As Jeff sat pessimistically beside Misti, I began asking her why she felt such a need to control Jeff. Misti responded that she really loved Jeff and wanted him to be the leader of the family, but she just wanted things to go a certain way and when they didn't, she found it hard not to take charge. After her answer, I had Misti recall her comments about her mother and how Misti couldn't wait to get away from her control.

"Misti, why do you think your mother was such a controller?" I asked.

"Well, I don't know."

"Did you like it, Misti?"

"Of course not, that's why I wanted to leave home," she responded curtly.

I then challenged her, "Well, if you didn't like the control of your mother, why should Jeff feel any different with your controlling him? Tell me what you think is the difference between your efforts to control Jeff and your mother's efforts to control you."

Misti's response was quick and defensive. "I'm not as bad as my mother!" she said as tears welled up in her eyes. With that, Jeff sat up on the edge of his seat and pointing his finger at Misti he said, "You're as bad as your mother and grandmother, Misti; you just don't realize it."

At that point I directed Jeff's attention away from Misti to cool things off. "Jeff," I asked, "why don't you tell me what you think of Misti's mother and grandmother."

Jeff was more than willing to give his opinion. "I hate being around Misti's family. Her father and grandfather are miserable in their marriages because their wives control them, but they won't stand up to them. All of the women in Misti's family are controlling. Even her sisters control their husbands, but her mother and grandmother are the worst. I've just made up my mind that I'm sick of being controlled by Misti and I'm not going to wind up like her father," Jeff stated as he sat back defiantly in his chair.

"Misti, what do you think about what Jeff just said?" I

asked.

With tears now streaming down her face and with broken-ness in her voice, Misti said, "Jimmy, I know I'm like my mother and grandmother and I hate it. I've always been so angry at the way they controlled and manipulated me, and now I'm doing the same thing to Jeff, but I don't know how to change. I'll do anything to change. I just don't want to lose Jeff, and I don't want to be like my mother."

The good news about Jeff and Misti is that their marriage was healed, and they are doing well. Misti was willing that day to begin to confront the sins that were handed down to her by her mother. Misti broke the power of the iniquities of control and manipulation from her life that day and remained faithful to her commitment to change. The result was a dramatic change in her life and in their marriage. Jeff also had iniquities and problems he was willing to deal with.

Because our parents' behavior affects us so directly, we as individuals must respond properly to our sins and problems. If we don't, the results are lifelong manifestations, which will damage our lives and will be passed on to our children. If we do, we can be free from the sins of our parents and pass that freedom on for many generations to come. Therefore, the remainder of this chapter will show you how to recognize iniquities in your life and in your parents and how to be set free from them as well as how to stop them from influencing your children. Here are the five steps to being set free from iniquities.

Step One: Recognize.

The first step in breaking iniquities is in learning to recognize the iniquities of your parents. The principle is pretty simple. An iniquity is any form of behavior you recognize in your parents' lives or family history as being unbiblical, not representative of the character of God, and which has had or is having a generational influence.

The following is a list of common iniquities people deal with: anger, gossip, prejudice, bitterness, judgmentalism, unforgiveness, chauvinism, dominance, sexual abuse, substance abuse, pride, fear, negativity, control, manipulation, physical abuse, irresponsibility, rebellion, verbal abuse, moral impurity, anti-social attitudes and behavior, co-dependent behavior. This list could fill pages, but the point is this: When you recognize the fact that you have been influenced by a negative trait in your parents, the first thing to do is to call it what it is. Freedom begins with truth.

Step Two: Forgive.

The second step in being set free from iniquities is to forgive our parents. After having recognized the fact that their parents are wrong, some people never become free because they refuse to forgive. In Matthew 6, Jesus reveals a powerful truth related to forgiving others. *"For if you forgive men their trespasses, your heavenly Father will also forgive you.*

> *After having recognized the fact that their parents are wrong, some people never become free because they refuse to forgive.*

But if you do not forgive men their trespasses, neither will your Father forgive your trespasses" (Matthew 6:14-15, NKJV).

Jesus tells us simply and directly that if we don't forgive the sins of others, our sins won't be forgiven. Without a forgiving spirit, freedom is impossible. In fact, unforgiveness is one of the worst forms of bondage. When Misti was still bitter and unforgiving toward her family, her life was spiraling downhill. However, she received a great healing and freedom in her life when she forgave her mother, father, and grandmother. That healing is blessing her marriage and child in a profound way.

Besides qualifying ourselves for God's forgiveness, another reason we need to forgive our parents is because in many cases they, like us, have been influenced by their parents in a negative way. Many people realize they have been negatively influenced by their parents, but never extend the same realization to their parents. If we carry baggage into adulthood and parenthood because of our past, doesn't it make sense to think our parents did the same? Misti's mother was controlled all of her life by her grandmother. The result was a woman who controlled her husband and children in an unhealthy way. Even though Misti was angry with her mother, she was following in her exact footsteps. When Misti realized this, she found empathy toward her mother that helped her to forgive.

In counseling over the years, I have come to realize that if I know about a person's parents, I can normally tell them with pretty good accuracy about their grandparents. People are always amazed when I do it, but it really doesn't take much skill. When you realize the fact that we are deeply influenced by our parents, then you realize that children are reflections of their parents. Extending this to our parents, we must realize many of their problems, sins, and hang-ups are the reflection of their family history.

In forgiving your parents, you must extend to them the same grace you want to receive from God. Name your parents' sins, and then forgive them and bless them. This is the beginning of freedom. I realize for some of you who have come from a past of serious abuse, the advice I have just given may be very difficult. Even though I understand that and sympathize with you, let me tell you this: It will be much more difficult for you if you don't. The only way you can be set free from the pain of your past is to forgive and let go. Only God has the understanding of one's family that it takes to be the judge. Therefore, we must put our parents in His hands and release them from our judgment. The most powerful effect of this takes place when we are able to pray for and bless our parents, whether they are alive or dead, thereby setting them, us, and our descendants free from a chain of generational sin and suffering.

Step Three: Repent.

Once you have completed the first two steps, the next step is personal repentance. Even though our parents may have wrongly influenced us, we are nevertheless responsible for our behavior. If our parents were critical people who never praised us, we must first forgive them. Second, we must personally repent for the same behavior in our life. Examining ourselves in light of our parents' lives, we must ask ourselves the sobering question, "Am I like them?" If we are, even in a different or lesser fashion, we must repent before God and others we have harmed through our behavior.

The only reason sin destroys families the way it does is because we fail to recognize it and deal with it properly. However, if we will call sin what it is, forgive those who have sinned, and repent for our own sins, the blood of Jesus then erases the power of that sin from our lives. A healthy examination for every parent is to consider what things we are doing with our children that could become an iniquity for them later on. If we notice that we are sinning toward our spouse or children or demonstrating unrighteous behavior before them, the answer is to repent before them and God. This has the powerful effect of stopping sin from further influencing our families.

Step Four: Submit.

The next step in gaining freedom from iniquities is to submit ourselves to Jesus. Iniquities begin as parents rebel against God's authority and the truth of His Word. The resulting sin twists and distorts their children's lives and perception of life. Once we realize this has happened to us, the cycle can only be broken by recognizing the original sin and making things right.

Once we have identified the sin, forgiven our parents and family, repented for our behavior to God and others, we must then ask Jesus to heal and change that area of our life. For Craig, this would mean asking God to teach him how to treat people of a different race. For Misti, this would mean allowing God to teach her how to change things and influence her home in a righteous and genuinely submissive way. For all of us, it means taking the wounded, bent areas of our lives to Jesus. As we submit to the authority of His Word and Spirit, the result will be true restoration for us and for many generations to come.

Step Five: Pray.

In Matthew 16, Jesus issued this powerful decree: *"And I will give you the keys of the kingdom of heaven, and whatever you bind on earth will be bound in heaven, and whatever you loose on earth will be loosed in heaven"* (Matthew 16:19, NKJV). Through prayer, we have incredible power over the unseen realms around us. The final step of freedom from iniquities comes by a spiritual decree to "bind" the power of any generational sin over our lives as well as our children and any future generations. This prayer also includes the "loosing" of the power of the blood of Jesus to cleanse our lives and to allow the Holy Spirit to empower and restore us.

Even though some might think this last step to be unnecessary or a little weird, it is nevertheless powerful to break the final cords of sin from us, which are the spiritual forces that work against us (Ephesians 6:12). Satan's demonic forces work constantly through generational sin to keep it operating and growing from one generation to the next. Their worst nightmare is the truth of God's Word and the power of His Spirit working in a believer's life to cut the umbilical cords of sin which tie them to their sinful past and feed their children's future with more of the same. The believer's prayer of "binding" sin and "loosing" righteousness is a powerful force God honors. I've prayed prayers like these hundreds of times for myself and others, and have seen true results.

The real power over spiritual forces was gained for us by Jesus on the cross. The second chapter of Colossians describes for us the incredible victory Jesus won for us over Satan and the powers of darkness. By the blood of Jesus, we are now enabled to overcome every force of hell as it seeks to come against us and to hold us in bondage. By faith in the finished work of Jesus on the cross and the power of His blood, we are able to pray with confidence, knowing that our prayers are answered.

One Final Word

For every parent reading this chapter, I hope you realize how powerfully your behavior affects your children. I hope this doesn't create any type of condemnation or unhealthy fear.

However, I do hope it creates an awareness of the awesome responsibility you have as parents toward your children. Your attitudes and behavior either reveal or distort God's character to them. It either creates a healthy environment where your children can grow up properly, or it creates a "wind of sin" which will bend them improperly.

There is no sin you or your parents have committed that God will not quickly and graciously cleanse if it is dealt with honestly. Right now, consider taking a pad of paper and listing the possible iniquities of your parents. After you have done that, make a list of which of those you recognize in your own life. Then go back through the list, forgiving your parents for their sins and repenting for your own. If you will do this with a sincere and honest heart, you will notice a powerful change in your life. Sins from your past that have had an anchoring influence upon your life will loosen their grip. Unseen chains that have held you back from God's best will be snapped as you are free to explore a new life, free from the iniquities of your past.

Psalm 51:5-7: *"Behold, I was brought forth in iniquity, and in sin my mother conceived me. Behold, You desire truth in the inward parts, and in the hidden part You will make me to know wisdom. Purge me with hyssop, and I shall be clean; wash me, and I shall be whiter than snow"* (NKJV).

Inner Vows: Promises of Bondage

Chapter 4 Jimmy Evans

St. Louis, Missouri—1962

The first chill of winter was in the air as Betsy Pratt pulled into her driveway. She could see her two daughters playing in their yard, which was meticulously manicured. Even though the Pratt family existed on Russell's modest salary from the bank, they nevertheless lived with great order and dignity. In fact, both Betsy and Russell had dreams of a better life one day when Russell would be promoted at the bank or maybe even get a better job somewhere else.

As Betsy got out of her car, she yelled across the yard to her two daughters, Jo and Dianne, to come and help her carry in the groceries. Jo, who was eleven years old and very mature for her age, came quickly across the yard toward her mother. However, Dianne, who was nine years old and a complete tomboy, pretended not to hear her mother as she continued to draw squares on the end of the sidewalk with a piece of blue chalk.

Struggling from the backseat with two sacks of groceries in her arms, Betsy Pratt carefully handed them to Jo for her to carry into the house. As Betsy turned back to the car for another load, she caught Dianne out of the corner of her eye as Dianne sat humming to herself with her back turned to Betsy. With the knowledge that her daughter was intentionally ignoring her, Betsy stomped down the sidewalk in an exasperated rush.

Grabbing Dianne by the shoulder of her favorite sweater, she pulled her to her feet. "Why didn't you come when I called you, young lady?" Betsy spoke sternly to Dianne as she started toward the car.

"Mom, stop pulling on me," Dianne shouted as Betsy began pulling even harder. "You're embarrassing me, Mom. Stop it!" Dianne cried out as Betsy increased the pressure on Dianne's arm.

"When I tell you to do something, you do it! Do you understand me, young lady?" Betsy barked rhetorically. "As soon as you get these groceries in the house, I want you in your bedroom doing your homework. And when you're finished, I want you back in the kitchen to help me with supper—and no talking back!" Betsy added. With a swat on Dianne's rear, Betsy left her standing in the driveway by herself as she headed for the front door. "Get it done now and don't break anything," Betsy spoke over her shoulder as she disappeared through the front door.

Dianne stood by the car wondering how she could have gone from having fun to being in trouble in such a short amount of time. As she bent over to look into the backseat, she was overwhelmed at the number of grocery sacks that were there. Finally, getting two sacks into her arms, Dianne began walking to the front door. With a complete sense of frustration, Dianne uttered these words to herself, "I'll never make my kids do this! I'm going to let my kids play, and they won't have to work."

Dallas, Texas—1994

Dianne and Rob Jenkins parked their car quickly as they both jumped out and hurried toward the door of the middle school. Their son, Jeff, was participating in an annual ceremony at the school where he was to receive an award for football. Jeff was thirteen years old and had always been a good athlete. Although not terribly interested in academics, Jeff was an active kid who loved sports and the outdoors.

Dianne and Rob hurried in the back doors of the auditorium just a few minutes before Jeff got his award. As they got settled into their seats in the back row, they could hear the names of some of Jeff's friends being read out loud by their football coach. The tenth name read was Jeff's. This was a proud moment for them as Jeff walked across the stage to receive his award for best defensive player of the year. Dianne and Rob squeezed each other's hand as Jeff sat back down with his friends.

After ten more minutes of the program, the principal of the school concluded it and dismissed the audience. Dianne and Rob stood and started looking for Jeff so they could get him as quickly as possible and go home. Dianne and Rob moved slowly and uncomfortably up the main aisle of the auditorium to try to get Jeff's attention.

After moving about twenty feet up the aisle, Rob felt a hand patting him on the shoulder. Looking back, Rob saw Jeff standing behind him with his friend Michael Lewis. Pulling Dianne around by her hand, Rob turned quickly toward Jeff and Michael. "Hi, Michael," Rob and Dianne said politely.

"Hey, Son, congratulations! We're proud of you," Rob said to Jeff as he shook his hand and patted him on the shoulder.

Dianne pushed her way past Rob and hugged Jeff warmly and said, "We're sure proud of you. You deserve your award, Honey."

"Thanks, Mom and Dad," Jeff said as he cut his eyes and smiled toward Michael. "Hey, listen. Michael wants me to spend the night and go with him and his brother tomorrow to the Grant High School football game. Can I go, please?" Jeff asked as he tugged on his mother's arm.

"Well, Jeff, I'm sorry, but you promised you were going to help me paint the house tomorrow. Remember, you want to buy roller blades, and you told me you would help me." Rob spoke as he patted Michael on the shoulder. "Maybe it'll work out next time," Rob said softly as he started moving slowly up the aisle.

As Rob walked away, Jeff turned to Dianne and began pleading. "Please, Mom, talk Dad into letting me spend the night. Please! Michael really wants me to stay over, and Coach Carey wants us to go to the game. I'll earn the money some other time. Please, ask Dad!"

With an affirming glance toward Jeff, Dianne said, "Wait here, Son. I'll talk it over with your dad." As Jeff and Michael celebrated the news, Dianne turned and followed Rob outside of the auditorium. Once outside, Dianne walked quickly to catch up with Rob until she could grab his arm and get his attention. "Honey!" Dianne spoke as she reached to take his arm. As Rob looked around, Dianne pulled his arm hard enough to stop him.

Once stopped, Rob turned and said, "What? Where's Jeff?"

"Well, he and Michael are waiting in the auditorium," Dianne answered. "I told him I would talk to you about him spending the night," she continued. Immediately Rob's eyes dropped as he let out a deep breath and got ready for what he

Jimmy Evans & Ann Billington   **Freedom From Your Past**

knew was going to be another fight with Dianne.

"Dianne, I told Jeff that if he promised to help me paint the house, he was going to have to do it. You never make Jeff or the girls do any work around the house, and when I try to get them to do something, you won't back me up. The answer is no; I'm not going to let Jeff out of it; he is going to do it," Rob stated as he folded his arms.

"These kids shouldn't have to work like this around the house. They're just kids," Dianne came back defensively.

"Yes, and they're irresponsible kids!" Rob responded. "It's time they learned to work around the house like I did when I grew up."

As Rob said those words, the fire ignited in Dianne's eyes. Not knowing what he had said to make her so mad, Rob knew that Dianne was about to do what she had done so many times in taking their son's side over his. As her chin trembled, Dianne took a step back and before turning away said, "I'm not going to let you ruin Jeff's life. I'm going back in there to tell Jeff he can spend the night and go to the game tomorrow, and I don't care what you say!"

As Dianne threw her body around and started back into the auditorium, Rob turned and began to walk quickly toward his car. In a daze, Rob knew his marriage with Dianne was at a breaking point. Even though he was attracted to Dianne and admired many things about her, he was to the point of realizing he simply couldn't be a responsible father and be constantly usurped by Dianne's fearful doting.

The two stories you've just read have something in common. The young Dianne Pratt, who at nine years old swore she would never make her kids work around the house, and the grown Dianne Jenkins, who vigilantly protected her children from domestic responsibility, are the same person. The obvious connection between the life of the nine-year-old girl and the distressed forty-one-year-old mother is the vow Dianne took as a child never to make her children work like she did.

Vows or oaths like the one Dianne made to herself at nine years old when she was made to carry the groceries into the house are very common. "I'll never make my kids do this! I'm going to let my kids play, and they won't have to work." These kinds of statements are what we refer to as "inner vows." Most people make many inner vows to themselves throughout life. Even though some of them have a more damaging effect than others, almost all inner vows have an unhealthy effect on our lives. In fact, some are very destructive.

Even though the statement young Dianne made might seem typical or innocent, it nevertheless had a lasting impact upon her life and future. Having once sworn to herself never to make her children do the kind of work she endured as a child, she was then obligated to fulfill that vow. The result was a marriage on the brink of divorce because her irresponsible children used her to avoid accountability or responsibility, despite every attempt by their father to change them. The emotional framework was erected when Dianne made that

> *Most people make many inner vows to themselves throughout life. Even though some of them have a more damaging effect than others, almost all inner vows have an unhealthy effect on our lives. In fact, some are very destructive.*

inner vow to herself at nine years old.

Another example of inner vows is from a friend of mine. When he was young, he became frustrated with his parents because they never had enough soda pop around the house. One day in total frustration with the fact that he couldn't find a soda pop to drink, he made the statement to himself, "When I grow up, I'm always going to have plenty of soda pop around the house for me and my children!"

Again, this statement may have seemed innocent enough. However, at thirty-five years old, my friend was still zealous in his commitment to fulfill his vow. Whenever he or his wife went to the grocery store, they loaded up on soda pop. If they ever came close to running out, he would strongly complain to his wife about not having any, and even if it meant going at an inconvenient time on his own, he made sure they always had soda pop. The health concerns of his family or the emotional state of his wife after being corrected for not keeping it in stock were both secondary issues. His primary concern was to not break the vow he had made as a child.

The two examples I've given so far are relatively mild. In more extreme examples, people swear things like this:

- "No one will ever hurt me again!"
- "I'll never be vulnerable again to anyone."
- "I'm never going to be poor like my parents!"
- "I'm never going to allow myself to fall in love with anyone ever again!"
- "I'm never going to trust anyone else in my life."
- "I'll never let anyone else make a fool out of me again!"
- "I'm not going to be strict with my children!"
- "I'm going to give my children everything they want."
- "My husband/wife will never treat me like that!"

These kinds of statements can set people up for a lifetime of dysfunction and misery. Behind the most bizarre and destructive behavior lie comments from the past like the ones you've just read. In helping people find freedom in their lives, it is very common to find one or more strong inner vows that must be broken.

In discussing the danger of inner vows and how to be set free from their damaging effects, I will first give you a definition of inner vows. Second, I'll show you scripturally why they're wrong. Finally, I'll show you how to break them from influencing your life any further.

Definition Of "Inner Vows"

An inner vow is a self-oriented commitment made in response to a person, experience, or desire in life. The key issue in understanding and identifying inner vows relates to the "self" nature of the vow. Whenever we focus a commitment inward, on ourselves, as opposed to upward or outward, that commitment becomes an "inner vow." Rather than freeing us from a problem or propelling us forward in life, inner vows act as tethers that perpetually hinder us and tie us to the past in an unhealthy way.

The Danger Of Inner Vows

There are three major problems that arise from the presence of inner vows in our lives.

Inner vows are unscriptural.

Here is what Jesus says to us in the fifth chapter of Matthew related to the vows we make: *"Again you have heard that it was said to those of old, 'You shall not swear falsely,* <u>*but shall perform your oaths to the Lord*</u>*' [underline mine]. But I will...*

say to you, do not swear at all: neither by heaven, for it is God's throne; nor by the earth, for it is His footstool nor by Jerusalem, for it is the city of the great King. Nor shall you swear by your head, because you cannot make one hair white or black. But let your 'Yes' be 'Yes,' and your 'No,' 'No.' For whatever is more than these is from the evil one" (Matthew 5:33-37, NKJV).

The main problem with an inner vow is the fact that it does not have to submit itself to God. Jesus tells us to *"...perform your oaths to the Lord."* This simply means that if we are going to make any significant commitments in our lives, they are to be focused toward God and fulfilled as an act of worship and obedience to Him. Inner vows are the exact opposite. Made to ourselves, inner vows are self-focused, self-serving commitments that in many cases resist and oppose the will of God in our lives. It is possible for a Christian person to live his entire life with four or five major inner vows operating under the surface of his consciousness, while living with the impression that he is completely submitted to the Lord.

To be set free from inner vows, we must first understand that we don't have the right to make vows to ourselves. If we are sincere in our walk with the Lord, this means that whatever comes into or goes out of our lives does so under the Lordship of Jesus Christ. To make an inner vow is to wrestle control of one's life from God and to set one's own course without His approval or blessing. This very point explains

> *Made to ourselves, inner vows are self-focused, self-serving commitments that in many cases resist and oppose the will of God in our lives.*

why so many inner vows cause so much pain for the person who made them.

Related to the unscriptural nature of an inner vow is the fact that inner vows are always tied to a "judgment" one has made. As you will find out in the next chapter, judgments also have a powerful influence in connecting one permanently to the negative issues of the past. Until judgments are broken and inner vows are renounced and submitted to God, we simply won't find the peace we are looking for in life.

Inner vows have an unforeseen effect.

When an inner vow is made, a course has been set for one's life. Even though we many times don't spend the bulk of our day thinking about all of the inner vows we've made, they nevertheless have a powerful influence upon us. As unseen forces that guide one's destiny, inner vows have the power to pull the strongest person in a direction he many times isn't even aware of. Part of the reason is because inner vows also have a "sleeper" effect. After having been made, they can become a part of one's subconscious mind until something happens to trigger them.

An example of this point was Dianne. Even though she didn't even know why she defended her children like she did or even why she got so angry at Rob when he tried to make the kids become responsible, it started when she was nine years old. The vow she made to herself on the way into the house with groceries was still silently guiding her life thirty-two years later.

One of the most dangerous things about inner vows is that when they are directing our lives, God isn't. In order to give the Lord true authority over our lives, we must first of all make sure there are no inner vows working silently beneath the surface of our thoughts, competing against the Spirit of God.

Inner vows are the most powerful level of commitment.

When it comes to what a person is going to do with his life, it typically comes down to his priorities and values. Most people value their own inner vows above their commitment to God. Inner vows are the highest level of commitment for most people.

Obviously, this isn't the way it should be. Our greatest commitment should be to the Lord. However, when we've sworn to ourselves that we will do something or not do something, subconsciously that commitment overrides any commitment we have to God. This point explains why there are so many precious, sincere Christians who say they love God, but have so many areas of their lives operating in such opposition to His purposes. Without even realizing it, they are fulfilling a commitment of their past which has unfortunately become a competitor with Christ.

As believers we must be careful not to let anything get in the way of our commitment to Jesus Christ. If we realize there are any commitments we've made to ourselves and withheld from God, we must quickly submit them, lest they keep us from fully giving ourselves to the Lord and serving Him in truth.

An example of the power of inner vows is from a man I knew whose wife came to me for counseling. This couple had a strong marriage and great children. The main reason this woman was in my office was because her husband was involved in a church that she and the kids hated. According to her, it was the "deadest, most boring church in the world."

Even though her husband agreed the church was lacking, he refused to leave. After twenty years of marriage, she wasn't contemplating divorce or anything like that, but she was seeking my counsel on whether she and the kids should seek another church environment while he stayed at the old church.

> *When you recognize specific judgments and resulting vows you made to yourself while growing up or even as an adult, renounce the inner vow and repent to God for taking charge of your life.*

As we talked about her husband's attitude about leaving the church, I found out something interesting. Rather than being raised in a dead church like the one he was in now, her husband had been raised in what she described as a "wild, holy roller" church. His parents were both leaders in the church. They took their children to services and events several times a week. As a youth, her husband strongly resented the strictness of his parents and the social stigma he had to endure because of his church background. One day, sitting with his parents in the fourth night of a five-day revival, her husband made this vow: "When I grow up, I'll never go to a church like this again!" After hearing that, I could understand why her husband had such a strong commitment to stay in his "dead" church.

I recommended four things to her related to her situation: Stay with her husband in the church; urge him to go for counseling; pray fervently for God to change his heart; and involve herself and her children in some good Bible study or church events beyond their Sunday morning experience so they could be spiritually fed.

How to Unlock Inner Vows

The first key to unlocking inner vows from your life is to think back on any failures of your parents in your past or any other negative life circumstances. As you are remembering, think about what your response was. Did you make certain promises to yourself about God, relationships, money, pain, or anything else? Did you make strong judgments about your past, your parents, or things relating to your future?

When you recognize specific judgments and resulting vows you made to yourself while growing up or even as an adult, renounce the inner vow and repent to God for taking charge of your life. Then take the area of your life in question and submit it to God. If there is a change to be made, ask God to reveal that to you. If you know what you have experienced is wrong, ask God to teach you how to do it properly. However, the main point is that your responses or commitments in life are not to be directed to you, but to God.

In unlocking our inner vows, we must release our judgments and unforgiveness for the people in our past. For Dianne, this means changing her judgment concerning children working around the home and her unforgiveness toward her mother. Almost all inner vows go back to some level of judgmentalism and unforgiveness. Even though it is necessary for us to make many assessments of people and situations throughout our lives, they don't have to result in unhealthy attitudes and self vows.

In every victory and in all suffering, God waits to help us and bless us. Whenever we reject the wise counsel and grace of God in the events of our lives, we are making a terrible mistake. Inner vows, no matter how innocent or seemingly meaningless, are direct threats to the Lordship of Christ and His will for our lives. They threaten to distract us from God and pull our loyalties away from Him and toward our own self-governing agendas.

Dianne and Rob sought marriage counseling, which saved their marriage. During counseling, Dianne realized the judgment she had put on her mother growing up and the resulting inner vow. Realizing that her selfish and sinful inner vow was keeping her from allowing her children to become responsible, as well as allowing Rob to be a responsible father, Dianne renounced her inner vow and submitted herself to Jesus and to Rob. The result was a transformed marriage.

Have you made any inner vows that are silently steering your life today? If you have, recognize them and break them. Even if your inner vow has a positive and healthy commitment attached to it, it should be made to the Lord, not to yourself. As you honestly examine your own heart and break the inner vows from your past, you take one more step toward becoming free from the unhealthy events and memories of your past—free to fulfill God's will for your life.

The Law of Judgments

Chapter 5 Ann Billington

How could it have happened? I had planned carefully, acted deliberately, and thought everything through before I married my husband. I had determined in my heart that I would never marry a man like my father. Over the years as I had observed my father, I had decided he was distinctly lacking as a parent. By escaping into sports, television, the newspaper and his work, he had remained uninvolved with the rest of the family. Now, years later, my attentive, sensitive husband worked six days a week, developed a love affair with the newspaper, and was addicted to television as he entertained himself by watching nonstop sports programs.

Where did I go wrong? When my husband and I first met, his personality was nothing like my father's. Unlike my father, he was fun-loving, energetic, communicative, and attentive. Yet, there he was in front of the television set, staring with

> In the beginning
> when God created
> the heavens and the
> earth, He created
> a complex world
> governed by a set of
> both physical and
> spiritual laws.

glazed eyes at another college football game. Little did I realize that his behavior changes were to some degree my own doing. Years ago I had judged my father as being an inept parent and, in doing so, had violated a spiritual law that would later return to haunt me.

Before we continue, let's take a moment and examine some foundational principles governing spiritual laws. Spiritual laws are a part of God's character. In the beginning when God created the heavens and the earth, He created a complex world governed by a set of both physical and spiritual laws. Adam and Eve were charged with the task of taking dominion over the earth and subduing it. Before sin entered, Adam and Eve were fully capable of governing the world by utilizing and understanding the laws ordering the spiritual and physical creation.

They were equal to this task because they were triune beings: body, soul, and spirit, with their spirits communing daily with the Lord. However, following their fall because of sin, the situation changed considerably. Not only did mankind degenerate, but the world itself began to decay. Man lost his capacity to dominate and rule an errant and deteriorating planet. In addition, man suffered a spiritual death, which rendered him unable to walk and talk with God in the intimate manner previously available to him. Through these altered spiritual conditions, man lost touch with the spiritual laws governing the world.

Today, physical laws such as gravity and thermodynamics are widely accepted. However, we need to understand that spiritual laws, though unknown by fallen, unredeemed man, are also in effect regardless of one's knowledge or faith in them. The eleventh chapter of Genesis provides an excellent example of a spiritual law at work in a pagan people. After the flood, man gradually migrated to an area called the Plain of Shinar in present-day Iraq. Having a common language, mankind united with the single purpose to build a tower to heaven.

For an ancient civilization dating to a period after the flood (roughly 2500 B.C.), this would seem to be a task far beyond its technical expertise. Yet, according to Genesis 11:6, God didn't take the situation lightly. In fact, He said, *"Indeed, the people are one and they have one language and this is what they begin to do; now nothing they propose to do will be withheld from them"* (NKJV). What was God's concern? He recognized immediately that the people of Babel had inadvertently stumbled on the spiritual law of unity. Therefore, nothing they set their minds to would be impossible.

It's not difficult for us to comprehend the nature of physical laws. The law of gravity will function whether you believe it is valid or not. If you jumped from a thirty-story building with a firm conviction in your heart that gravity would not prevail, you would still be dead after you hit the ground. These physical laws work without regard to a person's faith. The same principle is in effect with spiritual laws. As illustrated at Babel, the spiritual condition and degree of faith of the individuals has no bearing on whether a spiritual law is operational.

Approximately 2500 years after God's judgment on the people at the Tower of Babel, Jesus died and was resurrected to sit at the right hand of the Father. Because of this momentous event, redeemed man was reunited in spirit with the Lord.

With this union, man was once again equipped to tap spiritual knowledge previously denied him.

Let's go back to the story concerning my father and the spiritual law I violated—the law of judgments. I resented my father for working six days a week, 12 to 15 hours a day, coming home, withdrawing behind a newspaper, watching television, or simply refusing to communicate with us. Also, if there was a church or family outing, he would frequently decline. As a result, I resented my father's antisocial behavior and judged him for it.

Upon meeting my husband, I knew I had succeeded in finding a man as unlike my father as possible. However, after being married a short time, it appeared that my husband underwent a change. His basic temperament began to take on new traits I had never observed before. With each passing day, these traits resembled my father more and more. As I found out later, much of the change in my husband's life was a result of my violation of the law of judgments.

To help you better understand the concept of the law of judgments, three Scriptures reveal a great deal about the subject. Romans 2:1 reads, *"Therefore you are inexcusable, O man, whoever you are who judge, for in whatever you judge another you condemn yourself; for you who judge practice the same things"* (NKJV).

This Scripture informs us that when we judge another, we are promised condemnation. The point of Romans 2:1 is that we are not in a place to pass judgment on any person regardless of whether they are good or bad, saved or unsaved. Likewise, Luke 6:37 states, *"Judge not, and you shall not be judged. Condemn not and you shall not be condemned. Forgive, and you will be forgiven"* (NKJV). Judgment and condemnation are promised for those who persist in judging and condemning others.

Matthew 7:1-2 takes the violation of the law of judgment a

step further: *"Judge not, that you be not judged. For with what judgment you judge, you will be judged; and with the measure you use, it will be measured back to you"* (NKJV).

All three passages use the Greek word *krima* for the word *judge* which means "to judge, avenge, condemn, or legally pass sentence." This word implies more than assessing behavior. It carries with it the idea of assessing a value judgment on an individual, not simply on his actions. Judgment of this nature is an act reserved only for God. He is the only one in a position to judge a sinner. When we pass judgment on the individual, we set ourselves in the place of God, usurping both His function and authority.

In Matthew 7:1-2 it is also important to understand the Greek word for measure, *metron*, which means "rule, the degree, or standard." So, with the same standard of measure we use to judge others, we also will be judged by God in return. In verse two, the words "to measure back" come from another Greek word, *antimetreo*, which means "to measure back in return." Now, when you put all of this together, these verses take an interesting turn. They tell us not to judge, condemn, or place a value judgment on someone because God will return to us His judgment with the same measure we have used.

Understanding the Nature of Unrighteous Judgments

Jan and Steve both have family members who practice a homosexual lifestyle. Jan aches because someone she loves is involved in this sin. Steve, on the other hand, will not tolerate being in the same room with his family member because he cannot stand gays. These contrasting responses to the sin of homosexuality illustrate the difference between assessing sin and judging a sinner. We can recognize homosexuality as a sin, pray for the people involved, pray for deliverance, and plead for God's mercy on them. All of those responses are healthy and righteous.

Steve's position is not only to denounce the sin but also to condemn the sinner. Jan's position is to love the sinner but hate the sin. Steve is judging the person in a sinful manner and is therefore violating the law of judgments.

The Hidden Danger of Judgments

At this point in the process of placing unrighteous judgments on others, another powerful spiritual law begins to take effect—the law of sowing and reaping. Galatians 6:7-9 says, *"Do not be deceived, God is not mocked; for whatever a man sows, that he will also reap. For he who sows to his flesh will of the flesh reap corruption, but he who sows to the Spirit will of the Spirit reap everlasting life. And let us not grow weary while doing good, for in due season we shall reap if we do not lose heart"* (NKJV).

To understand the tremendous danger of judgments, it is essential that we comprehend several powerful principles which are at work in the spiritual law of sowing and reaping. The first principle is that whatever you sow, whether good or bad, will come back to you. With our actions and deeds, we are planting seed. We must understand that this means, with certainty, that sometime in our future there will be a harvest from that planting.

Thirty-two-year-old Jason came to my office seeking help for drug abuse. Jason wanted help, but he didnt want to change his lifestyle. He wanted to break the drug addiction but was uninterested in paying the price that change frequently requires. Not long after our meeting, he was arrested for drug dealing. When I visited him in jail, he was temporarily repentant and contrite. Later he was convicted and sent to prison for two years. Upon his release, he returned to his former lifestyle and activities, believing this time he would not be caught.

Jason remained out of jail three months before being apprehended on drug charges as well as forgery. So far, Jason has returned to prison four times. He can't understand that the "wages of sin is death" and that a man who sows sin reaps the consequences of that sin in his own life. It is an irreversible, universal, and eternal law of God. No one is exempt.

The second powerful principle of the law of sowing and reaping is that of multiplication. The harvest or return will be greater than the seed planted. If you plant one kernel of corn, you don't expect to reap only one kernel of corn. On the contrary, you expect a stalk with several ears of corn, each containing hundreds of kernels. So, whether we sow to our flesh or to our spirit, we can expect a significant increase at the harvest.

Years ago, when I was a teacher in a public school, a friend of mine went to happy hour with several co-workers. Since this woman was both married and a Christian, her presence there was certainly surprising. Sin entered one evening when she drank excessively and awakened the next morning to find herself in bed with a man who was not her husband. Her sin multiplied until within one year, her marriage was destroyed; she and her husband were in bitter dispute over the children, and each was prepared to destroy the other in court. What was sown

> *The second powerful principle of the law of sowing and reaping is that of multiplication. The harvest or return will be greater than the seed planted.*

one night in a bar ended in a holocaust of bitterness, hate, and marital destruction that changed the course of many people's lives forever.

Conversely, when we sow seeds of blessings, those, too, will be reaped in our lives. An example of the positive power of sowing and reaping is the story of a girl named Pam. For years Pam worked with teenagers, first at a summer camp as a college student and later as a junior-senior high school teacher. She had the privilege of becoming involved in the lives of countless young people and watching God do great things in them. Years later, Pam's son developed problems personally, socially, and academically. The onset of the problems were traced to a grade school teacher who verbally abused, not only Pam's son, but other students as well. By the time Pam became aware of the difficulties, the problems had escalated to an alarming level.

Pam decided to remove her son from public school and place him in a private school. Here he had a divine appointment with a veteran Christian teacher who bathed him daily in love, blessings, and prayer. The child that emerged at the end of this experience didn't resemble the same child who had experienced defeat earlier. Pam had sown good seed in the lives of others, and years later she reaped a harvest of blessing for her son. God's promise is that everything we do, whether good or bad, will be returned back to us. Pam's blessings weren't just an accident; they were the result of a law she accessed for the good of her life and her son.

The third principle of the law of sowing and reaping is that harvest has its own timing. All seeds have different germination periods. Some seeds will germinate within weeks, while others will lie dormant beneath the surface of the ground until soil conditions, temperature, and water are conducive to growth. Likewise, seeds of judgment may germinate quickly, or they may lie dormant beneath the surface of your life, awaiting just the right conditions to produce a multiplied harvest.

This principle is important to understand since it relates to problems we encounter many times as adults, which can in reality be traced back into our childhood or long ago in our adulthood. Sowing and reaping isn't always an instant process. Sometimes, the negative things we are experiencing today can be something which began years ago with seeds which were ignorantly or sinfully sown and have never been dealt with. We don't need to be hypervigilant about every event in our lives and what we might have done long ago to cause it. However, we do need to real- ize the long-lasting and delayed power of certain judgments and to be sensitive to something we might have done in our past which could be paying negative div- idends today. Also, this truth reminds us that whatever we do today can have long-lasting results into our future.

> ... seeds of judgment may germinate quickly, or they may lie dormant beneath the surface of your life, awaiting just the right conditions to produce a multiplied harvest.

The fourth and last principle of sowing and reaping is that good fruit cannot come from bad seed, nor can bad fruit come from good seed. Seed bears fruit in relation to its own kind. Luke 6:43-44 says, *"For a good tree does not bear bad fruit, nor does a bad tree bear good fruit. For every tree is known by its own fruit. For men do not gather figs from thorns, nor do they gather grapes from a bramble bush. A good man out of the good treasure of his heart brings forth good; and an evil man out of the evil treasure of his heart brings forth evil. For out of the abundance of the heart his mouth speaks"* (NKJV).

Good seed produces a good harvest, and bad seed a bad harvest. It's fascinating to observe how many people sow bad seed and expect blessings in return. In a sense, they believe they can take dandelion seed and produce a rose garden. There are also many who believe they can sow bad seed and expect no harvest. This thinking is foolish.

Recently, George and his wife, Jenny, came in for marital counseling. Both were Christians, and they had been married twenty-two years. Jenny had just informed George that she wanted a divorce. She wasn't involved with another man. She simply was sick of their marriage, and in her mind it was finished. As their story unfolded, it was one I had heard all too often. George was nonrelational and married to his job. He worked at least six days a week for an oil exploration company, putting in a minimum of twelve hours a day. He wasn't interested in relating to his wife, and he desired sex at his convenience. Because of George's work schedule, he spent little time with the children, seldom seeing them except on Sundays.

George was an absentee father and husband, deriving all self-image, self-respect, and identity from his work. When Jenny finally said, "Enough," George was astounded. He saw himself as misunderstood and betrayed because he believed he had been a faithful husband and a good provider. What George didn't see was the bad seed he had sown for twenty-two years. Now, he was reaping the harvest of his neglect and poor leadership.

Though George planted good seed by his faithfulness and provision, he didn't comprehend that good seed doesn't offset twenty-two years of bad seed. George was one of many who believe that good seed automatically neutralizes bad seed. This mentality causes many men and women to justify their faults and weaknesses. However, regardless of how deceived one may be, the truth remains that bad seed is present and grows in power the longer it is sown and allowed to remain in a person or relationship.

Another example of how the seeds we sow bear fruit in relation to their own kind is the story of a woman I knew who deeply resented her mother. According to this woman, her mother was the most critical and negative person in the world. She not only resented her mother, but also avoided being around her because she knew her mother would constantly criticize her and put her down.

Even though it is completely understandable why the woman would feel the way she did about her mother, she went beyond hurt and frustration into judging her mother. One couldn't be around her for long without hearing her say something sarcastic or negative about her mother. In fact, the longer I knew her, the more negative and judgmental she became about everything. Before long, she was just like the person she described her mother as being. Even more, she began to have many of the same problems with her daughter that her mother had with her.

In sowing seeds of judgment on her mother's criticism and negativity, she was insuring a future crop of reaping what she had sown. Because the law of sowing and reaping says we will reap according to what we have sown, she reaped a negative spirit from the negative seeds she had sown. Therefore, she became just like what she hated in her mother.

This is a dynamic of the law of judgments that we must understand. When we call someone by a name or make a value judgment on them, we will soon begin to feel the pull to become like what we have judged. This happens because we have set a law into motion that has tremendous power. God has promised in His word that we will reap according to what we have sown. Therefore, when we sow a seed through word or action, it will come back on us.

Like the story of the woman whose mother was negative, many of us become just like what we've judged in others without even realizing it. Even when we do realize it, we scratch our heads in disbelief that we could end up this way. Children often do this concerning their parents. They judge their parents for their problems and failures and then grow up to repeat them. We must understand the fact that when we judge someone for being or doing something, we tie ourselves to them and their condition through our judgment. We are then fed from that point forward by an invisible umbilical cord with the same spirit as what we have judged.

> When we call someone by a name or make a value judgment on them, we will soon begin to feel the pull to become like what we have judged.

To keep this from happening to us, we must realize the incredible power of the law of sowing and reaping. We simply will not escape the influence of this law. However, we can use the law to our advantage as we are careful in the seed we sow throughout life, making positive investments as much as possible.

Another important issue related to the danger of judgments and the power they have to bear fruit in our lives has to do with the combination of judgments and inner vows. The last chapter on inner vows discussed the way many people swear they will or will not become like their parents or someone they have judged. The main example used in the chapter on inner vows was Dianne, a young girl who judged the work ethic of her mother as too demanding; she later turned out to be the opposite type of mother when she enforced a weak standard of responsibility for her own children.

What we need to understand about judgments is the fact that they produce an intoxicant within our souls that won't allow for proper maturity and development. When we judge someone, we will either end up just like them or just the opposite, which is almost always as destructive and wrong as what we have judged. The person who judges, regardless of whether he combines his judgment with an inner vow or not, is like a drunk person trying to mount a horse. Falling from side to side, he will never be able to find balance and victory until the intoxicant of judgment is removed.

I counseled a man who was a weak leader in his home. His wife dominated the home, but complained often about his weakness as a leader. In counseling, we discovered that as a boy this man observed the dominant behavior of his father. One day as he watched his father verbally assault his mother, he made the statement to himself, "I'll never treat my wife like that!" Living true to his judgment and inner vow, he became the opposite of his father. Even though it was a positive thing for him not to be dominant like his father, he was locked on the opposite side of the issue, failing to fulfill his role as a leader. Once this man broke through the judgment he made concerning his father and forgave him for his mistakes, he was able to become the leader he needed to be.

The law of judgments insures that the judgments we make on others will return to us. The sowing and reaping principles guarantee that the seeds of judgment will produce a harvest of judgments in our lives. Furthermore, the harvest has its own timing. Judgments we make on others may return quickly in our lives or lie dormant, only to plague us later. In addition , we cannot issue judgments against others and expect something different or nothing at all to return. Perhaps the most dangerous element of the combined laws is that of multiplication. The judgments sown today will return multiplied in strength and number.

Considering the power behind the law of judgments, Christians would do well to judiciously assess the words of their mouths and the attitudes of their hearts as they observe the lives of those around them. If I had been more gracious with my father earlier in my life, the law of judgments would have produced a more appetizing crop for me. Unfortunately, because of my severe judgment on my father, I began reaping a bitter harvest in my marriage.

All of us have placed judgments on others. In fact, after judging others, many of us have become just like those we judged. If we haven't seen the negative effects on our lives from a judgment, it's not because we've escaped the law, but because either we haven't recognized the cause of the results, or the harvest hasn't born fruit yet—but it will. However, there is a way we can stop and even reverse the law of judgments if we have made mistakes.

Stopping the Curse of Judgments

Once we understand the power of the law of judgments, most of us realize we have made some serious mistakes. The question is, how can we stop the judgment on our lives from our mistakes and reverse the curse of the negative things we have spoken?

The first thing we need to do is to realize our sin. Have we judged people in the past—parents, brothers, sisters, friends, strangers? Are we judgmental people? Do we tend to make value judgments on people or types of people? We must learn to recognize that we have made judgments. God's word is clear about the fact that making judgments is a sin and the penalties are sure and serious.

The second thing we must do, after we have recognized our sin of judging others, is to repent to God. The sin of judging others is a sin against God before it's a sin against the other person. God is the only One who is qualified to judge someone. He knows people's hearts and judges them from an internal, eternal perspective and not just from externals the way we judge so often. To stop the curse of our own judgments from coming back on us, we must renounce an arrogant, judgmental attitude and commit to trust God to make the judgments necessary in the lives of others.

Third, after we have repented, we must break the judgment. This simply means that we undo the curse we have spoken with our mouth as we verbally renounce it. It would sound something like this: "In the Name of Jesus, I break the judgment I placed on my father. I repent for judging him for being detached and uncaring. I repent for the unkind things I said about him and the attitudes I displayed toward him. I now break the judgment I placed on my father from affecting him or me as I commit to love and pray for my father. Lord, forgive me for the sin of judging. Cleanse me and kill the negative harvest I have sown with my lips. Give me Your strength to change and to begin today to plant a crop of blessing and righteousness. In Jesus' Name, Amen."

Once we have broken the judgment, there is only one step left. The final step in breaking judgments is to remain true to what our lips have said. We can't break judgments and then turn around and continue to be angry, critical, and judgmental to the same person. Breaking the judgment must also carry with it a breaking of the judgmental attitudes within us. If this has truly happened, it means we will love people instead of rejecting them. We will pray for people rather than gossiping about them. We will say things to people to encourage them, rather than speaking hateful things behind their backs. We will lift up those who are downtrodden, rather than passing them by with an attitude of superiority.

Examining our past in light of the law of judgments is a wise thing to do. Ask the Holy Spirit to reveal to you any judgments you have made about others that would be coming back upon you today or will be coming later. Once you begin to humbly open up to the process of breaking judgments you have made in your past, you will begin to break a tie to your past that has the potential to damage your life today and your hopes for a bright future.

Once you have taken care of the past, the best investment you can make for your future is to use the power of the law of judgments on the side of blessing. When you are quick to repent for judging others and refuse to judge them, God will bless you. Even better, if you sow words and deeds of blessing into the lives of those God has put around you, you are sowing an incredible crop of happiness and security for your future.

"The heart of the wise teaches his mouth, and adds learning to his lips. Pleasant words are like a honeycomb, sweetness to the soul and health to the bones." Proverbs 16:23-24 (NKJV)

The Power of Unforgiveness

Chapter 6 Ann Billington

Holding a pitcher, bowl, and towel in his hands, my husband knelt beside the bed preparing to wash my feet. His bizarre behavior astounded me, as foot washing was certainly not a part of our daily routine. While he immersed my feet in water, he began a litany of repentance that shocked me. He openly acknowledged and repented for the oppressive, emotional, and verbal abuse he gave out for years and for the diabolical control and manipulation that laced our relationship. With tears spilling from his eyes, he recommitted to our marriage and family.

I had waited years to hear these words. This moment should have been a dream come true, but instead, I sat on the edge of the bed, and stared numbly at his bowed head. As he talked, I remembered. I remembered the violent fights, the episodes of rage, the expressions of fear and terror on our children's faces after the firestorm of hate had passed. I recalled the highway of pain that stretched behind us and loomed ominously in front of us. As far as I was concerned, our marriage ended years before; we just never signed the divorce papers.

As I observed the remorse mirrored on Jerry's face, I realized I felt nothing: no joy, no relief, no forgiveness. Resurrection power was needed to raise from the grave a heart that had withered and died long ago. I couldn't forgive, pick up the pieces, and go on as if the last ten years never happened. I knew what the Bible said about forgiveness, but knowing and doing were light years apart.

Somehow, it didn't seem right. I suffered in our marriage for years. Now Jerry was off the hook by simply apologizing. "I'm sorry" doesn't take away the pain that left me emotionally bloodied and wounded. I could have reciprocated. In response to his heart, I could have said all the right words, but words don't make it so.

Though Jerry repented, I continued to respond with cold indifference. Bitterness and resentment were resident in my soul. Quiet times with God became tortuous exercises in futility, as my prayers seldom seemed to rise past the ceiling. God's word had no life or breath in it. Restlessness invaded my spirit, and I became like a caged animal pacing the perimeters of my home.

Sleepless nights, inundated with fear and dread over unseen enemies, were my constant companions. As I slid deeper and deeper into the abyss, it became apparent that the power of unforgiveness was destroying me. That negative power was subverting my life. The question no longer was "How could I forgive Jerry?" but rather, "How could I afford not to forgive him?" Grievances I held against him became much less important in light of the destructive impact of my unforgiveness.

How do you change your heart? How do you move from

indifference to forgiveness—from hate to love? How do you forgive someone who has hurt you so badly it leaves you numb? How do you forgive someone who refuses to admit wrongdoing and persistently passes the responsibility to others? These and other questions are common for those embroiled in the task of forgiveness.

The Power of Unforgiveness

The first key to releasing genuine forgiveness is understanding the power unleashed by a failure to forgive. The sin of unforgiveness has a negative power that will adversely affect anyone who fails to forgive. In fact, once I realized the serious impact it had in my life, nursing hurts and bitterness seemed much less important.

> *The first key to releasing genuine forgiveness is understanding the power unleashed by a failure to forgive.*

No better story exists in Scripture to describe the power of unforgiveness than Matthew 18:21-35:

"Then Peter came to Him and said, 'Lord, how often shall my brother sin against me, and I forgive him? Up to seven times?' Jesus said to him, 'I do not say to you, up to seven times, but up to seventy times seven. Therefore the kingdom of heaven is like a certain king who wanted to settle accounts with his servants. And when he had begun to settle accounts, one was brought to him who owed him ten thousand talents. But as he was not able to pay, his master

commanded that he be sold, with his wife and children and all that he had, and that payment be made. The servant therefore fell down before him, saying, "Master, have patience with me, and I will pay you all." Then the master of that servant was moved with compassion, released him, and forgave him the debt. But that servant went out and found one of his fellow servants who owed him a hundred denarii; and he laid hands on him and took him by the throat, saying, "Pay me what you owe!" So his fellow servant fell down at his feet and begged him, saying, "Have patience with me, and I will pay you all." And he would not, but went and threw him into prison till he should pay the debt. So when his fellow servants saw what had been done, they were very grieved, and came and told their master all that had been done. Then his master, after he had called him, said to him, "You wicked servant! I forgave you all that debt because you begged me. Should you not also have had compassion on your follow servant, just as I had pity on you?" And his master was angry, and delivered him to the torturers until he should pay all that was due to him. So My heavenly Father also will do to you if each of you, from his heart, does not forgive his brother his trespasses"(NKJV).

First, unforgiveness has the power to separate us from God. Like the unmerciful servant who refused to forgive his

> Though unforgiveness doesn't cause us to lose our salvation, we do forfeit intimacy with God.

fellow servant and was thrust from the king's presence, we too are ejected from the favor of God when we refuse to forgive. Though unforgiveness doesn't cause us to lose our salvation, we do forfeit intimacy with God. It causes spiritually dry times, times when our prayers don't seem to go beyond the ceiling. God seems far away, and prayers have no answers.

No one can afford isolation from God. In the world in which we live, each of us needs all of Him we can have. John 16:33 tells us that while in this world we will have tribulation, but Jesus has overcome the world. We overcome only through Jesus, and we need the peace that comes with a right relationship with God and the confidence that He hears our prayers. That confidence comes with intimacy with God, which cannot occur in an atmosphere of unforgiveness.

Unforgiveness also has the power to hinder our sins being forgiven. In Matthew 18, the master forgave the unmerciful servant because he had compassion on him. Yet when the master learned of the servant's heartless behavior, he rescinded his decision and put the unmerciful servant in prison instead. In Matthew 6:14-15, Jesus says that our heavenly Father will not forgive our sins unless we forgive others.

I know a lady who was married for forty-six years. In the early years of her marriage, her husband's family flatly refused to accept her, saying that he had married beneath himself. To my knowledge, this lady never forgave her in-laws. She carried the unforgiveness to the grave. I wonder, did all of her sins follow her there? The Scripture plainly says God does not forgive us if we do not forgive others.

The negative power of unforgiveness is also the fuel that energizes bitterness and resentment, two forms of spiritual cancer. Once these cancers have taken root and residence in our hearts, we are vulnerable to everything from physical illness to emotional misery. Like all forms of cancer, bitterness and resentment spread to others. Many churches, homes, and families have been plundered and ravished by this spiritual disease.

Unforgiveness also has the power to generate a power failure in our lives. Love is our power source. It was the motivational force behind every act of God. Love fashioned the cross and gave us God's "only begotten Son." Likewise, as Christians we are to love our neighbor as much as we love ourselves. John 13:35 informs us that the world will recognize us not by our miracles, not by our church building, not by our doctrine, but by our love. Love is the foundational principle of the "good news of Jesus Christ."

While love is the foundation, faith is the element that taps the supernatural. It is by grace through faith that we are saved (Ephesians 2:8), by faith that we move mountains (Mark 11:23-24), and by faith that we are healed (Matthew 9:22). Just as faith is essential to walking in the supernatural, so is faith essential in love. Galatians 5:6 says that faith works through love, implying that love affects the workings of faith. Mark 11:23-25 also suggests a relationship between unforgiveness and ineffective prayer. So, as we pray to move mountains in our lives, we are instructed to forgive. Our faith only has power in a heart of love. In the absence of love, our faith doesn't work. Jesus' healing of the multitude was precipitated by love as He was moved with compassion for them. Likewise, the king in Matthew 18 had mercy on the unmerciful servant and released him from debt. Again, love was the motivating force behind the unmerciful servant's rescue.

Unforgiveness also has the power to blind our spiritual and mental eyes. True love and unforgiveness cannot coexist. When we choose love, we choose forgiveness. Conversely, when we fail to choose forgiveness, we fail to choose love. If we hold unforgiveness in our hearts toward another, we are not walking in love. According to 1 John 2:9-11, we abide in the light if we abide in love.

"He who says he is in the light, and hates his brother, is in dark-ness until now. He who loves his brother abides in the light, and there is no cause for stumbling in him. But he who hates his brother is in darkness and walks in darkness, and does not know where he is going, because the darkness has blinded his eyes" (NKJV).

If we fail to love, we stumble, not knowing where we are going. Perhaps the reason many of us seem to be stumbling through life is because we are walking in unforgiveness instead of love. We bump into troubles, difficulties, and crises because our lives are shrouded in darkness caused by unforgiveness.

Love flips on the light switch, enabling us to see clearly God's direction and plan. We can see problems and pitfalls. The alternative is to persist in unforgiveness, while navigating our lives through a labyrinth of difficulties and trouble, tripping and stumbling on our way to eternity, all because we don't turn on the light of love and forgiveness. Unforgiveness affects the power behind our faith and turns out the light necessary to traverse this life.

The Pain of Unforgiveness

The negative power released by unforgiveness also produces pain. Pain is something we all dislike. In fact, our natural tendency is to try to avoid it at all cost. Unfortunately, unforgiveness puts us in a prison of pain. The unmerciful servant's penalty for unforgiveness was prison.

I heard a story of a Vietnam prisoner of war who survived nine years in a Vietcong prison camp. His captors treated him inhumanely through frequent beatings and near starvation. The Vietcong isolated the prisoners in single, one-man cells, using loneliness as a method of control. The prisoner hungered for human contact, while boredom pushed him to the edge of sanity. The past consumed his imagination as he relived every memory, every hurt, and every joy. If the memories became too painful, he stayed the boredom by watching ants march across his prison floor or a bird build a nest in the prison window.

We, too, become prisoners of war when we allow unforgiveness to rule our lives. We become prisoners of the hurts and emotions of our past and are forever linked to the person or persons who injured us. Like the prisoner of war, we relive our past over and over in our imaginations, and the persons we will not forgive become our jailers. As long as I refused to forgive Jerry, I remained in a prison of pain, destined to endure again and again the hurts of the past. I wouldn't forgive and let it go. As I learned the hard way, as long as we live in the unforgiveness of the past, we have no future. We are linked to our past by invisible cords of pain.

A woman named Jane was sexually abused by her grandfather when she was three and for a number of years thereafter. As the family compared notes over the years, it appeared that Jane's grandfather abused every female in the family over three generations. Her grandfather died several years ago. She refused to attend his funeral. Had she attended, she would have spit on his grave.

Her grandfather received Jesus into his heart shortly before he died. Instead of rejoicing that her grandfather was in heaven, she was resentful. She much preferred that he burn in hell. Hell was what he deserved, considering the damage he caused over three generations. Jane was consumed with unforgiveness . It wasn't fair that he could spend his life destroying so many people, and then receive Jesus and not have to pay for it.

Jane is in a prison of pain, and her jailer, though deceased, is her grandfather. He might be physically dead, but he is alive in Jane's heart. She resurrects her grandfather each time she thinks of the abuse. Until Jane chooses to forgive, she will

Chapter 6 **The Power of Unforgiveness**

stay in her prison of pain, linked forever with the person she despises the most.

The pain of unforgiveness also produces the anguish of loneliness and isolation. No one can join us in our prison. Self-pity fuels the fires of loneliness, as we withdraw deeper and deeper into isolation. The prison cell of unforgiveness is only big enough for one. No one wants to follow us into our world of bitterness and disappointment.

Personal growth all but stops in our prison of pain. Unforgiveness inhibits personal growth, because we are blaming another person for our misery. Seldom, if ever, is a broken relationship entirely one person's fault. More often than not, each party within a conflict will bear a part of the responsibility. Frequently, one or both parties refuse to acknowledge their sin, opting instead to focus on the other person's problem. When an individual refuses to acknowledge his own sin, no change can occur. I find this particularly true with married couples. As long as one spouse is pointing at the other, each one's pride remains intact, and they don't have to change.

The walls of unforgiveness not only keep us confined to our past but also keep new relationships out. With unresolved issues, intimacy becomes an elusive dream. We withdraw, keeping other at arm's length, satisfying our hungry souls with surface relationships, destined to leave us unfulfilled and discontent.

> *The pain of unforgiveness also produces the anguish of loneliness and isolation.*

Finally, after years of failure, pain, and disappointment, we become numb. We no longer feel, as our walls of pain are replaced by our walls of denial. These walls keep us in and others out. Our world shrinks to the space behind the bars, distorting reality and truth and leading us into deception. Denial always blocks truth. Ultimately, we sit in our prisons, unfulfilled, unhappy, feeling little, wondering why we are failures in relationships.

The Punishment of Unforgiveness

The pain produced by unforgiveness should be enough retribution for anyone. However, beyond the pain, there is a promise of further punishment for those who refuse to forgive. Matthew 18:34-35 says, *"And his lord was very angry, and delivered him to the tormentors, till he should pay all that was due unto him. So likewise shall my heavenly Father do also unto you, if ye from your hearts forgive not every one his brother their trespasses"* (KJV).

Not only was the unmerciful servant cast into prison, but he was turned over to the tormentors . We, too, will be turned over to the tormentors if we refuse to forgive. The tormentors are demonic spirits who specifically attack the minds and hearts of those who are bitter. If we persist in unforgiveness, we open a door for demons to harass and attack us. Since we live in a fallen world in which Satan and his host are very active, opening the door to demonic activity is unwise.

The demonic oppression can manifest itself in a number of ways, such as depression, anger, confusion, or suicide. That isn't to say all depression, anger, confusion, and suicide are demonic or caused by unforgiveness. However, if unforgiveness rests in an individual's heart, it will become an open door which allows for such an attack. Having a clear understanding of the power, pain, and punishment of unforgiveness is a strong impetus for change. The backlash of unforgiveness is so serious that it is important to deal with it at all cost.

So, as I looked at the offenses Jerry had committed against me, I knew I had to resolve my unforgiveness before I could find peace. The problems associated with unforgiveness simply weren't worth the satisfaction of holding grudges.

Forgiving from Your Heart

For any spiritual truth to be effective, it must take root in our hearts. If it doesn't root in our hearts, it will never bear fruit in our lives. For example, Romans 10:9-10 says, *"That if thou shalt confess with thy mouth the Lord Jesus, and shalt believe in thine heart that God hath raised him from the dead, thou shalt be saved. For with the heart man believeth unto righteousness; and with the mouth confession is made unto salvation"* (KJV).

According to this Scripture, two things are required in order to be saved. The first is confession of the Lordship of Jesus, and the second is belief in your heart that He is the only true Messiah. Heart knowledge is more than intellectual assent. Satan knows that Jesus is Lord and that He was resurrected on the third day. He has intellectual assent to the facts. However, Satan certainly doesn't believe in Jesus from his heart. The same principle applies to unforgiveness.

Matthew 18:35 tells us clearly that God punishes those who don't forgive their brother from their hearts. Most of us know we should forgive. We know what the Bible says about forgiveness and we believe it. So, we attempt to forgive but discover it doesn't work. It doesn't work because we are forgiving from our heads and not our hearts. However, all heart knowledge begins with head knowledge that is committed to the process of becoming reality in our lives.

Regardless of whether you are the person who has been offended or you yourself have offended someone, the Bible gives specific directions about how God expects you to deal with bitterness and broken relationships. If you are the offended party,

> *Regardless of whether you are the person who has been offended or you yourself have offended someone, the Bible gives specific directions about how God expects you to deal with bitterness and broken relationships.*

the Bible says you must forgive. If you are the offender, the Bible says you must seek to be reconciled with your brother.

Matthew 5:23-25 elaborates on the process of seeking restoration in a relationship when you are the offender: *"Therefore if thou bring thy gift to the altar, and there rememberest that thy brother hath ought against thee; leave there thy gift before the altar, and go thy way; first be reconciled to thy brother, and then come and offer thy gift. Agree with thine adversary quickly, whiles thou art in the way with him; lest at any time the adversary deliver thee to the judge, and the judge deliver thee to the officer, and thou be cast into prison"* (KJV).

In this passage Jesus gives you four commands to obey if you know a brother or sister in Christ is offended at you.

Stop

Leave your offering at the altar. This means broken relationships can block your walk with God. Don't press further into spiritual pursuits until you make a sincere effort to be reconciled. This doesn't mean you have to be at peace with all men before you pursue God. It means God isn't completely pleased with your worship when you aren't concerned about broken relationships. Your efforts at restoration please God and make your offerings and worship meaningful. Remember, it was Jesus Himself who brought forth this important Beatitude in His Sermon on the Mount—Matthew 5:9, *"Blessed are the peacemakers, for they shall be called sons of God"* (NKJV).

Go

Take the initiative in the process of reconciliation. Prayerfully and peacefully seek to heal those relationships in which unresolved conflicts exist. Swallow your pride and overcome your fears.

Reconcile

Once you have located your brother, reconcile with him. The word *reconcile* in the Greek language means "to thoroughly change one's mind; to renew friendship." Even though you can't control another person's response toward you, you can do everything on your part to heal the relationship, trusting God to work.

Return

After reconciliation, return to God and spiritual pursuits. You will find an atmosphere of renewed spiritual vitality and freshness when you have been obedient to pursue restoration.

The Threefold Process of Genuine Forgiveness

Beyond restoring our relationships outwardly, there is the issue of how to achieve genuine forgiveness. When our emotions are volatile and we are angry, how do we find that place of true, meaningful release? In all forgiveness, regardless of whether it is mild or severe, there are three basic steps we must take to fulfill the biblical mandates of forgiveness.

Repent to God for unforgiveness.

The process of forgiveness begins as we repent to God for unforgiveness. Unforgiveness isn't just a problem; it is a sin against God. Because God is so gracious to forgive us, He is deeply offended when we harbor unforgiveness toward others. To be truly forgiving, we must first be truly repentant. The main way forgiveness transforms from being a decision of the mind to a posture of the heart is through an attitude of humility and brokenness, recognizing the seriousness of the sin of unforgiveness and the obligation we have to others because God's great grace forgave us.

Release the person from our judgment.

In order for true forgiveness to take place, we must release our offenders from our judgment. This means we make the decision to release them from our prison of judgment and revenge into the hands of God. For this release to take place successfully, we must let God be our avenger and their judge; we don't try to help Him in that process. For true release to take place, we must commit to never again slander them, talk bad about them, or seek revenge in any form. Release is a critical step in the process of forgiveness.

Once we have made the decision to forgive, the devil will always send one of his messengers into our lives to try to reignite our offenses. People around us may say things that could easily offend us. The person we release from our judgment may do something else to offend us. Regardless of what happens, we can't truly forgive until we truly release that person. We must expect challenges in this area anytime we are seeking to forgive. With an attitude of repentance and a commitment to release our offender to God and to follow through in our speech and behavior, we are well on our way to freedom.

We must bless our offender.

Here is what Jesus said in Luke 6:27-28: *"But I say to you who hear: Love your enemies, do good to those who hate you, bless those who curse you, and pray for those who spitefully use you"* (NKJV).

Once, I was working through a very serious problem with a person. I went for months without forgiving her. One day in prayer, the Lord reminded me about what He said in Luke 6 about blessing those who curse us. The Lord directed me to begin to bless the person at whom I was offended and told me the issue wouldn't be resolved in my life until I did. As I began to do this, I noticed an incredible peace and openness with God. Not only that, I began to feel genuine compassion for my offender.

One day in prayer as I was going through a mechanical recital of blessing for her, the eyes of my heart opened, and I began to see her through the eyes of God. At once I was filled with compassion as the bitterness disappeared. To my surprise, I could see a value in her and actually cared for her. Blessing not only penetrates the darkness of our emotions, but it also reestablishes a person's value to where it should be.

I believe the issue of blessing is the most powerful ingredient for changing our unhealthy emotions toward a person. When we have been damaged emotionally, it's hard to change the way we feel. Even if we've made the decision to forgive, the feeling doesn't automatically follow. However, when we begin to bless our enemies and those who have hurt us, it releases a blessing from God that overcomes our feelings and the enemies of our emotional healing.

When I first started trying to bless the person God had directed me to pray for, it was one of the hardest things I've ever done in my life. Not only were my feelings full of bitterness for the person, but also I really didn't want God to bless her.

However, I was obedient to bless her every day. Even though my feelings didn't change immediately, approximately ten days after I began blessing her, I received a major breakthrough. My bitterness was transformed into compassion, and my devaluing attitude toward her was turned to godly respect.

We must understand that God loves those whom we hate. Even though we might find one hundred reasons to despise them, God finds more reasons to love them. Blessing is an agreement with God's attitude and desire related to our enemies and those who have hurt us. Therefore, when we agree with God, He releases a great blessing upon us as well as using us to bring a permanent solution to the lives of our offenders.

The poison of unforgiveness damages the person in whom it is stored worse than anyone it can be spit upon. One of the most self-loving and beneficial things we ever do in our Christian lives is to forgive others. Don't let unforgiveness rest in your heart any longer. Commit yourself to the process of forgiveness for every person and event in your life you recognize as being out of the will of God. Also, be committed to the process of reconciliation as God's Word directs.

If you desire to forgive from your heart, begin the process. God will carry you through. Remember, nothing is worth separation from God. Nothing is worth the pain and punishment unforgiveness causes. On the other hand, it's worth everything you have to forgive. The blessings of forgiveness are great. Make a decision now to be a forgiving person. As you submit yourself to God, begin to confess to Him any areas of unforgiveness in your heart. The process of forgiveness will not only disconnect you from the poison of your past, but it will also guarantee a peaceful and blessed future.

The Scars
of Our Souls

Chapter 7 Ann Billington

Emotional and mental wounds are the scars of one's soul. They are the hurts of the three-year-old girl who was raped by her grandfather, the wounds of the boy who spent the night in his dad's pickup truck after his father passed out drunk behind the wheel. They are the wounds of the wife whose husband had an affair and wants a divorce. They are the wounds suffered through neglect, abuse, rejection, trauma, and divorce, to name a few. All leave an imprint of pain in the life of the individual, and that pain must be healed.

Because we live in a less than perfect world, it's impossible to live life without pain. Everyone experiences hurt and wounds to varying degrees. However, many are carrying wounds dating far back into their past. Unfortunately, time doesn't always heal. The hurt doesn't just go away. It must be repaired. As long as the wounds are untouched by God, they remain open, creating emotional infections that poison both our lives and our relationships.

We must understand that emotional and mental wounds don't heal like physical wounds. In the case of physical wounds, there is an immediate attempt by the body to heal itself. After a period of time, we are healed "naturally." However, our inner wounds aren't that way. The scars of our soul don't heal until we have allowed them to.

> We must understand that emotional and mental wounds don't heal like physical wounds.

I remember a man who came into my office for counseling. He was sixty-five years old. Ten minutes into our counseling session, he was crying and telling me what had happened to him when he was a six-year-old boy. Fifty-nine years later, this man was still being affected by the inner wounding of his heart as a boy. Fortunately, on the day he was in my office, he began to allow healing to take place.

Many people go throughout their lives with unhealed hurts. Like a person who limps because of a broken leg that has never been set, these people "limp" through life emotionally. Never able to reach their potential because of their emotional infirmities, these people must be careful not to let their fragile hurts be exposed or redamaged. In many cases, people with unhealed emotions project an exterior of strength and confidence. However, on the inside they are still hurting. If only they would allow the hurt to be healed, they would be delivered from their pain.

One of the foremost reasons people aren't healed of emotional and mental scars is that they are intimidated and scorned by others. An example was a woman I was counseling who had been raised by a mean, alcoholic father. Even though she was a precious lady, she had some serious emotional problems that haunted her all of her life. Every time she began to open up about her father and the abuse she endured, her husband would try to make her feel guilty because she was still bringing up the past.

I told her husband that she needed to bring it up in order to be healed. I patiently explained to him how our emotions are different from our physical bodies. Even after all of those years, she would continue to have emotional problems until she was healed. Thankfully, she received some deep ministry, and her husband supported her through the process.

Another important reason people have problems in receiving emotional and mental healing is that they do not know how to get help. Many people hurt deeply and would do anything to get help, but they just don't know how. So many sincere and willing people remain unhealed. This chapter is designed to give you some of the answers and the directions you need in order to learn how to be healed and to know from this point forward the correct path to take to receive emotional and mental healing when you need it.

The Danger of Denial

Hurting people sometimes go to great lengths to avoid pain. They employ an assortment of mental gymnastics to deceive themselves. Denial is the most common method used to derail hurtful feelings. The human mind has the incredible ability and power to deny not only the pain, but even the event that caused the pain.

I was sexually abused when I was three years old. However, my mind entombed those events. I had memory fragments dating to that time in my life, but never understood their significance. Throughout our marriage, my husband had remarked that I had all the signs of having been sexually abused. Since I had no recall, I steadfastly denied it. Then, six years ago, a series of events occurred that stirred my memory. One night, as I began to drift into the twilight of sleep, I remembered. Like pieces of a puzzle coming together, everything suddenly made sense. Had this recall happened to anyone else, I easily could have doubted its validity. However, the memory was real and for years had been suppressed. I am frequently astounded at the power of the human mind. It can take a memory and bury it so deep that the conscious mind is oblivious to it.

Denial also presents itself in other ways. Judy was a woman defecting from a satanic coven. She recounted tales of unending abuse, beginning from her earliest memory. As the saga of horror unfolded, she displayed no emotion at all. She had perfected the ability to divorce her memories from the pain. Denial was so strong that it became disassociation, a split between the event and the emotion. Consequently, she turned off all emotion.

Defensiveness is sometimes a form of denial. Many people are so bound by shame and pain that to admit wrongdoing is more than they can accept. Though the truth will set one free, some individuals would rather live a lie than look honestly at the truth.

Recently, I visited with a married couple whose marriage was in trouble. I allowed each one to tell their story, beginning first with the wife. As she inventoried her husband's failures and shortcomings, he offered no defense. Finally, it was his turn to share. After almost every point he made, his wife defended, denied, or excused her actions. She assumed no responsibility for her behavior, preferring to place all blame on her husband. This lady steadfastly refused to see needy areas in her life. Consequently, no significant change could occur until her eyes were opened.

Drug and alcohol abuse are another favored method to deny pain. Many individuals have so much unresolved anguish in their lives that they have anesthetized themselves with drugs or alcohol. Joan, who was a prescription drug addict, confessed to me that only when she takes pain killers does her suffering ease. Upon investigation, I discovered that she had abused drugs for fifteen years. Her goal was not to get high. Instead, barbiturates took the edge off of her emotional pain, making life manageable.

Denial can take many forms. Regardless of how it manifests, it blocks the healing process. Obviously, the truth cannot set one free if one refuses to accept it. Denial is a front line defense. If its walls are not broken down, the individual continues in his pain, generating counterproductive behavior and sin such as control and manipulation, anger, or obsessive performance. Though denial can be engineered by demons, more often than not, it's a coping mechanism designed to avoid pain and must be painstakingly countered with truth. The worst part of denial is that it prevents Jesus from healing the wounds from one's past.

The Process of Healing

Once a person is willing to face the reality and pain of his past and denial is overcome, a door is then opened to his emotions. Frequently, the next feeling a person experiences is anger. This anger is manifested in two different ways—either anger turned outward or anger turned inward. This anger can be very violent and explosive as the person recognizes the hurt that was previously covered over by denial now lying just beneath the surface.

Pat was a woman with a seemingly calm exterior. She

was controlled and even tempered. Pat's father had sexually abused her. When we discussed the abuse, she related the event dispassionately, maintaining the incident no longer troubled her. Pat had been married three times, each time to an alcoholic or drug abuser. She was the strength in all three relationships, giving and giving until she was emotionally depleted. She sarcastically and disgustedly characterized all men as weak, dependent "jerks."

I suggested that Pat study through a workbook on sexual abuse by Dan Allender, *The Wounded Heart.* A few weeks later, Pat returned to my office. Thunderous rage had replaced her calm facade, as the walls of denial crumbled and truth was exposed. Pat was furious at her father, whose selfishness set her life on a course of dysfunction and misery. God didn't escape her wrath either. If He "…was such a big and loving God, how could He allow things like that to happen to children?" Pat felt cheated out of a childhood, realizing there was no road back to lost innocence.

For most of her life, Pat devalued her feelings regarding the sexual abuse. She made excuses for her father, minimizing the experience. At other times, she assumed responsibility for her father's actions, believing there must have been something "bad" in her that encouraged his behavior.

In time, Pat's anger turned inward and manifested in self-hate. She wasn't ready to acknowledge the shame and rejection from her past. Instead, she raged, first at her father for being a selfish animal, and then at herself for being so weak and defective as to have allowed the abuse. Of course, Pat was a thirty-four-year-old woman looking back at an event that happened to an eight-year-old. She was judging an eight-year-old with thirty-four-year-old eyes.

Pat was a committed Christian who sought God even as she raged at Him. One morning during a quiet time, she felt compelled to read James 1:21-25:

"Therefore lay aside all filthiness and overflow of wickedness, and receive with meekness the implanted word, which is able to save your souls. But be doers of the word, and not hearers only, deceiving yourselves. For if anyone is a hearer of the word and not a doer, he is like a man observing his natural face in a mirror; for he observes himself, goes away, and immediately forgets what kind of man he was. But he who looks into the perfect law of liberty and continues in it, and is not a forgetful hearer but a doer of the work, this one will be blessed in what he does" (NKJV).

After reading this Scripture, she realized she had allowed her anger to pervert the character of God in her mind. Although she didn't fully understand everything yet, she recognized that she had turned away from the truth and had fallen into deception. She made a decision to stand on what the Bible said. She repented and released her anger and judgment toward God, herself, and her father. With that decision, the anger subsided and her journey of healing began.

Though Pat received a release through the Scriptures, not everyone in this stage of healing is as fortunate. One of the angriest people I have ever known was a man who was 6'4" and weighed about two-hundred-fifty pounds. He was calm most of the time, unless of course you crossed him. Then a cold, hard look entered his eyes which, with his size, could be intimidating. He sought help for his fits of anger.

He left home at fifteen because his father beat him. Now, as an adult, he resorted to anger at the first sign of opposition. It was a tool he used to mask his feelings. Even though his anger was a result of his past, it kept him from being able to heal and mature properly. Unfortunately, he didn't go on to receive emotional healing. He has remained angry at the world, blaming everyone else for his torment.

Anger is not necessarily a negative emotion. Ephesians 4:26 tells us that we can be angry, but not to sin in our anger. Anger is a normal and natural response to abuse and violation. However, anger must be appropriately expressed and ultimately released. For example, it is both normal and acceptable to feel anger towards someone you perceive has hurt you. However, to harm or abuse that person is an inappropriate response to your anger. Though the anger may be legitimate, the manner of release may not be.

Once you can articulate the reasons for your anger, you need to submit it to the Holy Spirit. Prayerfully, give your anger to God, asking Him to help you express it and discover the feelings it may be masking. Also, repent of any sinful behavior or bitterness your anger may have caused. Many people, like Pat, become angry at God or others, but refuse to acknowledge it. However, the anger is still present and is manifesting itself through unhealthy internal and external manifestations such as self-hate, depression, anger, bitterness, etc.

Also, regarding our negative feelings about God, many Christians believe anger toward Him is a terrible, unforgivable sin. Therefore, we often steadfastly refuse to admit it. Since God knows our every thought and feeling, we are only fooling ourselves by not being honest about it. Therefore, it is to our advantage to go ahead and confess our anger toward God and ask for His help and forgiveness. Anger toward God is not an unforgivable sin, and God lovingly receives our honest confession.

Once people release anger, they enter a grieving stage. During this phase, they may experience anguish deeper than they've ever known. These are the feelings they've feared and avoided. Jesus knows the wounds are there, but because of their denial or anger, He has been unable to reach them. He says in Revelation 3:20: *"Behold, I stand at the door and knock. If anyone hears My voice and opens the door, I will come in to him and dine with him, and he with Me"* (NKJV). Although Jesus knows their hearts and wants to heal them, He won't force an entry into a wounded heart. All doors of the heart open from the inside and must be released by the individual. For them to open these doors, they have to trust the Lord and be willing to walk through the issues of their lives with Him.

Pat entered this stage after her encounter with God. She reported pain so deep she felt that she couldn't breathe. Sometimes she could easily identify the issue of grief. Yet, at other times, she couldn't attribute the pain to a specific incident or problem; she just ached. There is very little that can be done during such times except to pray and trust God. Friends and family must be patient and supportive, allowing such a person to hurt and go through the stages of grief.

> We naturally want to take away a person's bad feelings. However, it is most important that the hurting person get in touch with his pain, feel it, and allow Jesus to heal it.

We naturally want to take away a person's bad feelings. However, it is most important that the hurting person get in touch with his pain, feel it, and allow Jesus to heal it. There are no short cuts in this process. One can't go around it, under it, or over it. Any effort to circumvent the healing course will delay the cure.

Pat grieved her losses for the first time in her life. Naked truth replaced illusions. She described it as a death. Gone were the excuses for her father and mother. The fantasy world created around her childhood crumbled, and in its place were broken dreams and harsh reality. Gone were the innocence of youth and a childhood she couldn't recapture. Together, we submitted every hurt, sin, and area of unforgiveness to God. Slowly and painstakingly the Holy Spirit touched each wound as Pat released forgiveness to those who had hurt her. As she grieved her way through the pain, Jesus healed her heart.

The grieving period is a critical time. It can seem overwhelming and frightening. The rush of pain is much like a dam breaking. As the structure collapses, water rushes through at a dangerous and alarming rate. However, as the water empties, the raging current shrinks to a tiny, quiet trickle. The thousands of pounds of pressure trapped behind the dam are now a gentle, free stream.

As the rush of pain subsides, the hurting person slowly moves into acceptance and resolution. The individual, like the gently rolling river, is no longer trapped behind a wall of denial, pressure, and stress, but is free to peacefully pursue his path down stream.

Psalms 55:4-8 says it well: *"My heart is severely pained within me, and the terrors of death have fallen upon me. Fearfulness and trembling have come upon me, and horror has overwhelmed me. So I said, 'Oh, that I had wings like a dove! I would fly away and be at rest. Indeed, I would wander far off, and remain in the wilderness. I would hasten my escape from the windy storm and tempest'"* (NKJV).

Our wounds are seldom inflicted by strangers, but most frequently by those we trust and love. A close friend scarred the psalmist's soul, making the wilderness an appealing refuge. Though David yearned to escape his pain, he instead turned to God. He encourages us to, *"Cast your burden on the LORD, And He shall sustain you; He shall never permit the righteous to be moved"* (Psalm 55:22, NKJV). Although David was overwhelmed, he was confident God would deliver him. It takes great courage to be honest and allow God to reveal the scars of your soul. Though it may hurt for a season, Jesus is faithful and will never leave you nor forsake you. If you realize you have wounds of your heart that need to be healed, consider praying this prayer:

"Jesus, give me the courage to face the scars of my soul. You know the deepest secrets and the hidden places of my heart. Break down the denial in my heart that causes me to see myself and others dishonestly. Give me clear eyes, Lord, to perceive the truth about my life. Forgive me for the sins I've committed by avoiding the truth. I cast the burden of my pain on You and trust You to sustain me. Please Lord, heal the scars of my soul and lead me to emotional and mental health. In Jesus' Name, Amen!"

When we come to the Lord with an honest and open heart, He can do anything. Even though there are times when the Lord does miraculous healings, in most cases the Lord chooses to heal us through a process. This process not only brings healing, but it also teaches us how to live our lives healed. Our prayer for you is that you would trust Jesus to walk you through your hurts. You can trust Him never to do anything in your life to harm you. On the contrary, Jesus will lead you to perfect healing.

Concerning His ministry to the hurting, Matthew 12:20-21 records this powerful Scripture: *"A bruised reed He will not break, and smoking flax He will not quench, till He sends forth justice to victory; and in His name Gentiles will trust"* (NKJV). These verses speak of the gentleness and care Jesus takes in dealing

> *Faith in God is what gives us the ability to dream of a place of quiet waters and green pastures, even while we stand in the midst of the valley of the shadow of death.*

with fragile lives. The devil wants us to believe God is disgusted with us and is far removed, up in heaven somewhere, far away from our hurts. The Bible reveals the opposite.

Jesus is intimately acquainted with our hurts, fears, and problems. He is the only one who can truly heal us and lead us through the valley of the shadow of death into the pastures of emotional and mental peace. In order for Him to do that, we must trust Him as our Shepherd and we must become one of His sheep. In receiving significant healing myself, as well as having observed hundreds of others receive their own, I can tell you without a doubt that the most important ingredient in receiving emotional healing is faith in God and His love for us.

Faith in the power and love of God is what gives us the ability to face our fears and hurts. Faith is what gives us the hope for tomorrow when our todays are filled with pain and heartache. Faith in God is what gives us the ability to dream of a place of quiet waters and green pastures, even while we stand in the midst of the valley of the shadow of death.

Trust in Jesus. Allow Him to come into the painful areas of your life. Be honest—totally honest—about yourself, your feelings, the past, and others. As you let Him walk with you through the places where your soul has been scarred, He will not disappoint you or hurt you. Rather, He will heal you forever so the places you are scarred today will rejoice tomorrow in His faithfulness.

> *"The LORD is my shepherd; I shall not want. He makes me to lie down in green pastures; He leads me beside the still waters. He restores my soul; He leads me in the paths of righteousness for His name's sake. Yea, though I walk through the valley of the shadow of death, I will fear no evil, for You are with me; Your rod and Your staff, they comfort me. You prepare a table before me in the presence of my enemies; You anoint my head with oil; my cup runs over. Surely goodness and mercy shall follow me all the days of my life; and I will dwell in the house of the LORD forever."* Psalm 23:1-6 (NKJV)

Exposing the Unseen Enemy

Chapter 8 Ann Billington

As a young Christian, I was taught that Satan was little more than a myth. In fact, I didn't believe God or Satan touched our earthly lives in any tangible way. I imagined their involvement with mankind was like a football game. Humans were the players, the field was life, and the spectators were all of the heavenly beings. The game kicked off at our birth; it then proceeded through the fumbles of failure to the touchdowns of success, all accomplished without the direct involvement of angelic or demonic spectators. When the final whistle blew, God tallied up the good and the bad and assigned each player his new eternal address. Therefore, prayer and other spiritual disciplines were Christian duties not expected to help much, while each one's future was left up to the uncertainty of fate.

I believed this until the night our two-year-old son, Dane,

began having night terrors. These episodes were more than bad dreams or nightmares; they were incidents of horror. One evening I was awakened from a sound sleep by bloodcurdling screams coming from Dane's room. By the time I dashed upstairs, Dane was standing in his bed, trembling, pointing at the corner and screaming, "It's going to get me." He trembled uncontrollably for hours.

Prior to these occurrences, we noticed that Dane refused to sleep or play in his room. He got out of bed off and on all night, frequently sleeping on the landing at the top of the stairs. At first, we ignored this behavior, thinking he just needed to adjust to his new surroundings. However, as time went on, we realized we were experiencing a dimension of reality that we didn't understand.

When we shared our experiences and concerns with our Bible study leaders from our church, they quickly confirmed our suspicions that we could be dealing with a spiritual entity and not just bad dreams. Soon after our conversation, they came to our house to pray for Dane. However, their prayers took an unusual twist. After petitioning God, they directly addressed Satan and his demons, commanding them to leave our home and cease their harassment. That night Dane went to bed, slept peacefully all night, and never again had a night terror, bad dream, or nightmare.

Some people don't believe Satan is a real being. They rationalize him away as a mythical character who was invented by uneducated and backward people. However, the Bible is very clear regarding his existence and purpose on earth. One of the clearest texts in Scripture related to the history and reality of Satan is Ezekiel 28:11-19 (KJV):

> *"Moreover the word of the LORD came unto me, saying, Son of man, take up a lamentation upon the king of Tyrus, and*

say unto him, Thus saith the Lord GOD; Thou sealest up the sum, full of wisdom, and perfect in beauty. Thou hast been in Eden the garden of God; every precious stone was thy covering, the sardius, topaz, and the diamond, the beryl, the onyx, and the jasper, the sapphire, the emerald, and the carbuncle, and gold: the workmanship of thy tabrets and of thy pipes was prepared in thee in the day that thou wast created. Thou art the anointed cherub that covereth; and I have set thee so: thou wast upon the holy mountain of God; thou hast walked up and down in the midst of the stones of fire. Thou wast perfect in thy ways from the day that thou wast created, till iniquity was found in thee. By the multitude of thy merchandise they have filled the midst of thee with violence, and thou hast sinned: therefore I will cast thee as profane out of the mountain of God: and I will destroy thee, O covering cherub, from the midst of the stones of fire. Thine heart was lifted up because of thy beauty, thou hast corrupted thy wisdom by reason of thy brightness: I will cast thee to the ground, I will lay thee before kings, that they may behold thee. Thou hast defiled thy sanctuaries by the multitude of thine iniquities, by the iniquity of thy traffick; therefore will I bring forth a fire from the midst of thee, it shall devour thee, and I will bring thee to ashes upon the earth in the sight of all them that behold thee. All they that know thee among the people shall be astonished at thee: thou shalt be a terror, and never shalt thou be any more."

From these verses we learn that God created Satan both wise and perfect in beauty. He was a covering angel to whom God gave full access to His presence. However, because of Satan's arrogance and rebellion, God cast him from heaven. "So the great dragon was cast out, that serpent of old, called the

Devil and Satan, who deceives the whole world; he was cast to the earth, and his angels were cast out with him" (Revelation 12:9, NKJV).

Though Scripture clearly reveals Satan's created existence, some people continue to relegate him to a mythical or comical character with a forked tail and horns. Possibly the greatest deception perpetrated on the human race is that Satan isn't real, but rather a figment of religious fanatics' overactive imaginations. If Satan can continue to discredit his own reality, he can continue to wreak unresisted havoc in the lives of believers and nonbelievers alike.

However, Satan is not a god, but he does have a kingdom that God and man allow him to rule. This kingdom is ordered in rank and file by demons of varying power. The fact that Satan's kingdom has an organization and structure of authority is revealed in the tenth chapter of Daniel. An angel sent to speak with Daniel was delayed three weeks by the Prince of Persia—a powerful demonic entity. So obstinate and powerful was this prince's resistance that it required a warring angel's intervention. Obviously, this particular demon was very strong, indicating that he held a high rank among the powers and principalities of darkness. Conversely, the angel speaking to Daniel didn't have sufficient power to break through the opposition by himself, but required the assistance of an angel whose function and power was superior to the Prince of Persia.

Ephesians 6:12 tells us that our struggles are not against flesh and blood but rather *"...against principalities, against powers, against the rulers of the darkness of this age, against spiritual hosts of wickedness in the heavenly places"* (NKJV). This Scripture suggests a distinct rank within the demonic kingdom, whose mission is to attack man and thwart the plans of God. So, not only is Satan a real creature, but he and his forces also attempt to attack and hinder us in our pursuit to follow God. Nevertheless, Satan and his forces are always subject to God.

In Jesus' earthly ministry, He regularly dealt with people who were oppressed by demonic forces (see Luke 6:17-18 or Mark 3:10-11). The Gospels give consistent accounts of Jesus casting out demons and setting people free from spiritual oppression as a regular part of His ministry. Jesus was the greatest minister of all times. He can't learn anything from Sigmund Freud. He didn't minister the way He did because He lacked technology or modern psychological discoveries.

Jesus ministered deliverance to people because demonic oppression was one of the sources of their distress. Without His ministry of deliverance, these people wouldn't have received the full ministry and freedom they needed. Most of those Jesus ministered to were normal people with problems, not demon-possessed maniacs.

We also need to realize that Jesus' biblical ministry wasn't just a historical record; it was a living example of how we can be set free and minister freedom to others today. Acts 5:16 tells us that one of the ministries of the early Church was the ministry of deliverance: *"Also a multitude gathered from the surrounding cities to Jerusalem, bringing sick people and those who were tormented by unclean spirits, and they were all healed"* (NKJV). Mark 16:17 records these words from Jesus Himself concerning the ministry of deliverance: *"These signs will follow those who believe: In My*

> *Most of those Jesus ministered to were normal people with problems, not demon-possessed maniacs.*

name they will cast out demons…" (NKJV). He also gave to those who believe, authority over all the power of the enemy, Satan (Luke 10:17-20).

Rather than considering the ministry of deliverance as weird, we must understand that it is real and needs to be accepted and understood. Without taking this truth too far or becoming fixated upon the devil, we must learn to address the issue of deliverance in a balanced and biblical manner. Satan or demons haven't left the earth or changed their nature in the past two thousand years. They are still here and still desire to attack us and hinder God's will for our lives. We must accept this reality and learn how to overcome them.

The Fourfold Method of Satan's Attacks

Satan and his demons attack man in four ways. First and possibly the foremost way he attacks man is through deception. Satan is a deceiver. John 8:44 says, *"You are of your father the devil, and the desires of your father you want to do. He was a murderer from the beginning, and does not stand in the truth, because there is no truth in him. When he speaks a lie, he speaks from his own resources, for he is a liar and the father of it"* (NKJV).

Genesis 3:1-6 illustrates Satan's powers of deception. In this account, Satan approached Eve by asking if God had indeed restricted them from eating the fruit of any of the trees of the garden. Eve quickly corrected the serpent by informing him that the fruit of all of the trees was available except the fruit of the tree of the knowledge of good and evil. The penalty for eating the fruit of that tree was death. The serpent quickly began to work his deception upon Eve by telling her that she would not suffer death if she ate of the fruit. In fact, not only would she not die, but upon eating it, she would become wise.

According to the devil, God was trying to keep Adam and Eve from a wonderful blessing. Satan's ploy was to cast doubt on God's love, faithfulness, and motives. Satan implied that God selfishly withheld the fruit of the tree of the knowledge of good and evil because He was jealously guarding His position. Satan clearly insinuated that God didn't really love Adam and Eve or have their best interest at heart, but was more concerned about competition and didn't want them to become a god like Him. Satan's attempt was to assassinate God's character. He was successful. Eve ate the fruit.

Today, as I minister to people and listen to their problems and hurts, the deception of the enemy becomes apparent. Mankind struggles under a load of guilt, shame, and condemnation. Many will go to their graves never knowing how much God truly loves them or that He desires their health and happiness.

Like in the garden of Eden, Satan and his host are still about their task of perverting man's image of God. He will tell the young man whose father beat him that God is sitting on His throne, holding a belt and waiting anxiously to thrash him. He will tell the woman who was raped that it was her fault and God was punishing her. The woman who was molested by her father, afterward believes she is dirty, shameful, and unacceptable to God. All are lies, perpetrated by the father of lies, to deceive and distort God's character before us.

Satan's first line of attack is deception. If he can deceive the world into believing in Buddha rather than Jesus, he has won a victory accomplished through deception. If he can persuade a Christian man or woman that God's love is unreliable, he can neutralize his or her willingness to trust in God or to energetically pursue Him. If he can convince the hurting that there is no hope in Jesus, he can sentence them to a lifetime of despair and dependency. All of these can be accomplished through the deception of the father of lies.

Occult activity is the second way of Satanic attack. As public awareness of ritualistic crimes has increased, so has public acceptance of an unseen world. The Christian recognizes the unseen world as the scene of a supernatural, spiritual battle between good and evil. Prayer is the vehicle through which the Christian talks to God and engages the enemy. However, many nonbelievers contact the supernatural world through occult practices and in so doing align themselves with Satan and his kingdom. Some of these practices are as follows:

- Ouija boards
- Palmistry
- Handwriting analysis
- Automatic handwriting
- Extra sensory perception (ESP)
- Hypnotism
- Horoscopes
- Astrology
- Levitation
- Fortune telling
- Water witching
- Tarot cards
- Pendulums
- Witchcraft
- White magic
- Black magic
- Conjuration
- Incantations
- Charms
- Fetishes

> *The Christian recognizes the unseen world as the scene of a supernatural, spiritual battle between good and evil. Prayer is the vehicle through which the Christian talks to God and engages the enemy.*

God warned the children of Israel to abstain from all forms

of witchcraft. Deuteronomy 18:9-12 says, *"When thou art come into the land which the lord thy God giveth thee, thou shalt not learn to do after the abominations of those nations. There shall not be found among you any one that maketh his son or his daughter to pass through the fire, or that useth divination, or an observer of times, or an enchanter, or a witch, or a charmer, or a consulter with familiar spirits, or a wizard, or a necromancer. For all that do these things are an abomination unto the lord: and because of these abominations the lord thy God doth drive them out from before thee"* (KJV).

Witchcraft in all of its forms is an abomination to God. Today, witchcraft has come out of the closet. The entertainment industry has saturated the market with rock music, movies, television shows, and books glamorizing the occult, with the single purpose of enticing people into occult activity. Participation in the occult is a slap in God's face and an assault on His love. Every believer should be careful to stay away from occult activity, no matter how popular or harmless it seems.

The third way Satan attacks our lives is through physical illness. Matthew 17:18 gives an example of a demon spirit causing seizures. Certain cases of muteness and paralysis in the Bible were also attributed to demons. In an age of increasing scientific progress, the idea that demons could cause physical ailments is considered medieval thinking. However, there are many examples of people who are healed when demonic spirits are bound and cast from their lives.

Lester was a successful attorney whose flawless professional reputation and personal integrity were widely recognized within the community. He came to the church seeking relief from migraine headaches. He was under the care of a neurologist who prescribed an assortment of very strong pain relievers. The medication dulled and slowed his mental processes, impairing his ability to practice law. Discontinuing the medication sharpened his mental faculties, but left him open to developing terrible headaches. The headaches completely incapacitated him for up to twenty-four hours and at times required hospitalization. In praying for him, I directly addressed the spirits of infirmity causing the headaches. The headache left within thirty minutes, a miracle in itself, and he hasn't had another headache for three years. Though the origins of migraine headaches may be many and complex, Lester's headaches were demonic attacks and responded to the authority of Jesus Christ.

The fourth way demons attack is through mental disorders. The classic biblical example is the Gadarene demoniac in Mark 5:1-6.

> *"Then they came to the other side of the sea, to the country of the Gadarenes. And when He had come out of the boat, immediately there met Him out of the tombs a man with an unclean spirit, who had his dwelling among the tombs; and no one could bind him, not even with chains, because he had often been bound with shackles and chains. And the chains had been pulled apart by him, and the shackles broken in pieces; neither could anyone tame him. And always, night and day, he was in the mountains and in the tombs, crying out and cutting himself with stones. When he saw Jesus from afar, he ran and worshipped Him. And he cried out with a loud voice and said, 'What have I to do with You, Jesus, Son of the Most High God? I implore You by God that You do not torment me.' For He said to him, 'Come out of the man, unclean spirit!' Then He asked him, 'What is your name?' And he answered, saying, 'My name is Legion; for we are many'"* (NKJV).

These verses describe a man tormented by unclean spirits.

Verse 9 says that the name of the spirit was Legion. This name reveals that about six thousand demons were occupying him. A great number of spirits drove this man to self-destructive, masochistic behavior. He lived among the tombs, crying out and gashing himself constantly. He also possessed supernatural strength far beyond that of an ordinary person. Obviously this demoniac was emotionally and mentally bound by demons.

Satan still oppresses people mentally and emotionally. Even though few are driven to the point of insanity like the Gadarene demoniac, at various times we all experience mental and emotional distress. Daily, I listen to people who contend with problems of self-esteem, fear, shame, insecurity, performance, and depression, to mention just a few. Frequently, I find that these problems are caused by demonic forces and can only be cured by taking direct authority over those spirits causing the problems.

Kathy complained of overwhelming fear. Night times were periods of terror for her. The fear was so strong and so present that it was like a physical weight lying on her body. Her heart palpitated wildly, while anxiety washed over her like a tidal wave. She either paced the floor or tried to sleep while clutching her Bible to her chest. Though there were other pertinent issues affecting Kathy, the spirit of fear oppressed and tormented her. After we prayed and took authority over demonic spirits of fear, she experienced a release unlike anything she had ever known. Until the spirit of fear was addressed, Kathy was paralyzed in her efforts to manage her life. Dealing with the demon of fear freed Kathy to work on other problem areas.

Performance and perfection were two troublesome spirits contributing to the mental and emotional problems of Sean. By his very nature, he was an orderly, methodical individual. In addition to his natural bent toward order, he was raised by a demanding parent who insisted on perfection. Obviously, most

> *Few mental and emotional disorders are entirely the result of demonic oppression.*

people with this background would struggle with performance and perfection. However, this man's entire life was controlled by these spirits.

Sean was driven by a compulsive need to succeed. The need for perfection and flawless performance consumed him. After commanding the spirits of performance and perfection to leave, Sean was able to manage these compulsive areas. Again, Sean had some serious problems related to his self-worth and identity that it took more than deliverance from demons to cure. However, these problems became much more manageable after the spirits left.

A caution should be presented at this point. Few mental and emotional disorders are entirely the result of demonic oppression. Ordinarily, they result from a variety of problems. However, since Satan's mission is to kill, steal, and destroy, the demonic element should never be ignored.

Satan and his hosts are most definitely real and affect man's mind, body, and emotions. Armed with this knowledge, we are now ready to address different levels of demonic oppression and how to personally deal with them. The next chapter will help us to understand even more the nature of spiritual forces and how to overcome those that would use our past, our weaknesses, and our sins as an entry way of destruction.

Freedom from Spiritual Oppression

Chapter 9 Ann Billington

On January 17, 1992, the world anxiously watched as President Bush ordered coalition forces to attack Iraq. For months, Saddam Hussein taunted the world as he challenged them to the "mother of all wars." The world witnessed technology that enabled our forces to "surgically bomb" a weapons factory, while leaving an orphanage next door intact. How did our fighter pilots know exactly which building to strike and which to leave unharmed? With the help of sophisticated spy satellites, the allied forces knew precisely which structures to take out and which to leave. As the war continued, it became clear that the allies had done their homework. They knew the enemy well.

Like the allied forces in operation Desert Storm, we would be wise to know our enemy, who day and night seeks our destruction. Therefore, this chapter is dedicated to helping us understand and overcome the schemes of Satan as he seeks to loose his demonic forces to control and ruin our lives.

Before we deal with the issue of how to detect and overcome demonic forces, we must first settle the question as to whether a Christian, as well as a non-Christian, can be possessed by demons. For years Christians have struggled with the issues of demons and demonic possession. This concept seems unbelievable and farfetched to many reasonable people. Beyond our ability to understand the issue in general is an age-old theological question over whether a Christian can be possessed. The argument against a Christian's ability to be possessed is based upon the understanding that a Christian belongs to God: mind, body, and spirit—making demon possession impossible.

To resolve this concern we must understand the correct definition of the word *possession*. What does it mean? Unfortunately, the King James Bible consistently renders the Greek word *daimonizomae* as *possessed*. Though this is one definition given by *Strong's Concordance*, it can also be rendered, "vexed with a devil; to have a devil; to be under the power of a demon." If we accept the definition as "possession," which implies ownership, a Christian most definitely cannot be owned by Satan because he is owned by God. However, if the word is more accurately rendered "afflicted," a Christian can definitely be afflicted and influenced by demons. Allow me to illustrate.

Imagine that you were a homesteader early in America's history who was taking possession of the land that the United States government deeded to you. However, upon your arrival you discovered a family already living on a small portion of your property. These individuals were called squatters, and you, as the homesteader, had the right by law to eject the squatters from your land. The squatters neither owned the land nor did they have complete control over it. Title deed belonged to you, the land owner.

Some of us find ourselves in a similar situation. The moment we accepted Jesus as our personal Savior, we signed the title deed of our life over to Him. The Bible reveals the fact that Jesus bought us with a price (1 Corinthians 6:20; 7:23). He owns us—we are His property. However, seeing us as His possession, Jesus realizes that squatters [demons] are trying to illegally occupy His property. They don't own the land, and they have no legal right to the territory they attempt to control. Knowing this situation exists in many of His people, Jesus wants us to realize the authority we have to eject demonic intrusion.

In gaining confidence to take authority over demonic oppression, we need to realize that every biblical example of so-called demonic possession reveals limited demonic power.

Take, for instance, the woman of Luke 12:1 who was affected by demons for eighteen years. From the account, the demons only affected her back. She was apparently fine in every other part of her body. Evidently, the demonic powers oppressing her were limited in their ability to influence her life.

Even the account of the Gadarene demoniac in the fifth chapter of Mark supports the idea

> *In gaining confidence to take authority over demonic oppression, we need to realize that every biblical example of so-called demonic possession reveals limited demonic power.*

of limited demonic power. He was definitely under significant demonic control, but it took a legion of demons to accomplish it. Since it took approximately six thousand demons to control the Gadarene demoniac, it proves that individual demons are limited in their ability to affect humanity. As squatters illegally inhabiting God's property, demons are limited both in their ability to influence our lives and their ability to resist when we confront them by the legitimate authority of Christ.

So, can a Christian be possessed by demons? No, Christians cannot be possessed. They are owned body, soul, and spirit by Jesus. However, they can certainly be affected by demons who are trying to illegally inhabit God's property. This is where our need to understand demonic power and God's authority over it is very important. To begin to understand demonic oppression, we will first explain the four levels of demonic activity. After that, we will deal with how demons gain entry into our lives, the four major hindrances to deliverance, and finally, the authority of the name of Jesus.

The Four Levels Of Demonic Activity

The first level of demonic activity is called suppression. This form of influence is low-key and somewhat weak. In fact, we would most often tend to pass it off as irritability or a bad mood. Of course, not every bad mood or irritable episode we experience is demonic. In fact, many of us will bounce back naturally. However, should the feelings persist for a long time or deepen in their influence, demonic activity should be considered.

The second level of demonic activity is called mild oppression. This form of influence is characterized by a deepening of demonic pressure. The moods, emotions, and general sense of oppression run much deeper. The individual is not incapacitated, but he is definitely struggling with control. For example, let's examine how the spirit of anger might behave. At the suppressive stage, anger would be controlled and might be expressed in irritability. In contrast, obsessive anger would become explosive from time to time.

The third level of demonic activity is severe oppression. At this point the individual is clearly in a significant struggle to control the affected area or areas of his life. He will experience frustration and even confusion as he tries to manage the fight within. If anger is the spirit manifesting, he may have frequent episodes of rage. If he is attacked by a spirit of depression, he may find himself experiencing lengthy periods of melancholy moods, seldom having a positive day.

To the person afflicted with severe oppression, it seems as if he will never have victory over his dilemma. He tries hard not to sin, not to be depressed or angry, but he fails again and again. Frequently, people at this stage report feeling as if another person is in control. When they return to "normal," they look back on the episode like it happened to someone else. In this stage, several demons are usually at work at the same time. Most of us need others to stand with us when this kind of activity is present.

A lady came to the office one day to visit with me regarding the strange behavior of her friend, Sharon. She was very concerned about the dramatic changes she had seen in her friend. Sharon had quit work to stay home and be a homemaker and mother, and since doing so, she had reported uncontrollable episodes of rage that erupted seemingly for no reason. She was also tormented at night by nightmares while unseen voices plagued her in the day. Paranoia and fear stalked her continually. The following week the lady brought her friend to see me. Upon investigation, I found that not only was Sharon experiencing all that had been reported, but also she related that the furniture moved on its own and drawers opened and closed at will. Sharon was experiencing severe demonic oppression. When I began to pray for her, she began to cry, wail, and moan. As the Lord gave me discernment, I commanded the demons to leave in the name of Jesus. This was a lengthy process as I called out each demon by name. When we finished, she collapsed on the sofa. This session was the beginning of her walk into freedom. There was a marked difference in her behavior within the first twenty-four hours. Several more sessions were required before full freedom in these areas was achieved.

The fourth level of demonic activity is possession—a condition not possible for Christians. There is a man in our city who wanders the streets day and night. Unkempt, he wears the same filthy clothes each day and stands on street corners having imaginary conversations with unseen people. He is clearly out of touch with reality and is controlled by unseen forces.

There are also those so steeped in Satanic religion that possession is clearly evident. Many of them admit they are possessed by spirit guides who have names and speak to them. Some have even given their souls to Satan and have asked him to indwell them. This level of demonic activity is extremely serious and requires concerted prayer and spiritual preparation before being confronted.

Open Doors For Demonic Assault

Since demons have limited power, they have limited access to our lives. In other words, they can't just jump on us. Ordinarily, they must take advantage of an opportunity—an open door. Sin is the main avenue demons use to enter a person's life. Unrepentant sin eventually becomes an access point demons take advantage of, which in turn allows the enemy legal ground for oppression. An excellent example of this is the sin of unforgiveness. As was discussed in chapter six, unforgiveness opens the door to tormenting spirits. Therefore, people and situations in our past who are still unforgiven also become openings to our lives for enemy infiltration. In fact, when people make the decision to forgive others against whom they have held a grudge for a long period of time, there is always an oppression lifted from them, accompanied by a sense of renewed peace.

Another open door to demonic activity are the sins of parents and how they affect their children. As parents, we are custodians of our children. We are to create an atmosphere of purity and safety in which our children can grow up properly. However, when a parent sins, it breaches the atmosphere of spiritual purity. The result can be demonic activity. The degree to which a parent sins and remains in sin is the same degree to which demonic activity can exist within and around the parent. Unfortunately, demons are vicious and will use the doorway the parent has opened to attack the children also. In reading this, you may be able to think about a particular sin of your parents while you were growing up. If you can, it may mean that you were and still are exposed to spiritual oppression as a result. The answer is to forgive your parents for their sin and take authority over the spiritual results in your life.

Chemical addiction is another classic example of repeated sin opening the door to spiritual oppression. Though there are many issues pertinent to addiction, demonic activity is definitely one of them. Few drug addicts ever predetermine in their minds that they will become addicted. It happens over a period of time with repeated sin.

I worked in a drug abuse clinic that treated heroin addicts. After a time, I noticed that all of the patients acted somewhat alike. It was almost as if the addiction had a personality, a pattern of behavior similar in each person. The peculiar thing was that the addicts didn't live together or interact with each other, nor did they have an environment in common. After considerable study we found that there was also no particular socioeconomic structure that produced addicts. They came from wealthy homes and poor homes, large families and small families, divorced homes and homes with both parents happily married. In short, the most common denominator among them was the drug. Understand, there are many problems faced by an addict that have nothing to do with demons. In fact, ministering to an addict is multifaceted and complex. However, within the addict's life, there are definite demonic entities that must be addressed.

Another doorway or inroad of the enemy is occult activity. This might be as innocent as ouija boards at a slumber party or as full-blown as Satanism, but every level opens doors for demons. Leviticus 19:31 says, *"Regard not them that have familiar spirits, neither seek after wizards, to be defiled by them: I am the LORD your God"* (KJV). God commanded the Israelites not to participate in any form of witchcraft. It is an abomination to God.

A man who was of Indian descent (Cherokee) visited me in my office. He had been raised on a reservation where he was baptized into the Catholic Church. Though he was Catholic, his mother and father still held to the old religious traditions of his ancestors. He recalled his mother frequently sending for the witch doctor whenever he was ill. The witch doctor used chants and charms to perform healing magic. Though he was only a child, this level of witchcraft rendered him susceptible to demonic forces. Later, as an adult, he developed mood swings, massive depression and erratic behavior, all of which ceased once the demonic was addressed.

Another situation involved a witch affiliated with a coven located in another city. She became fearful of the cult and sought refuge with us. Though she accepted Jesus as her personal Savior, she continued to complain of oppression. A friend and I went to her house and removed three grocery sacks full of occult material including a bible of witchcraft. After praying for her, she received an immediate release.

It is in the best interest of each of us to allow the Holy Spirit to take inventory of our lives to see if there has been any occult activity that might produce problems. (Chapter 8 has a comprehensive list of occult practices.) It is also important to remove from your house any occultic artifacts, jewelry, posters, music, or symbols, for they, too, can be an entry point for demonic spirits.

Another very common open door for demonic activity is one's physical or emotional trauma and hurts. I combine these because deep physical, mental, and emotional wounds are traumas in themselves. It appears that when a person undergoes shock or trauma, his conscious mind is weakened. During this time, the enemy will attempt many times to make inroads into his life.

When our daughter, Wendi, was eight years old, she was hit by a car. When I arrived at the accident scene, the horror of her injuries and the threat to her life overwhelmed me. The panic reduced me to a mindless robot moving only on command. I was in that state for several hours, waiting to see whether she would live or die. Thankfully, she lived, but I emerged from the experience changed. A mindless, unreasoning fear and terror gripped me. I couldn't control it—it controlled me. I became phobic over the safety of my children. If they didn't return home from school exactly when I felt they should, panic consumed me as I jumped in my car to look for them.

This condition continued to worsen until it became crippling for me as well as for my children. Finally, a dear Christian lady prayed for me to be released from a spirit of fear and it was instantly gone. I believe the trauma surrounding Wendi's accident so neutralized my mind that it left me temporarily open for a demon of fear to attach itself. To say I have never known fear since that time would be absurd, but I haven't known that overwhelming, paralyzing, crippling fear brought on by that event.

Evidences of demonization are broad and cover almost every area of a person's mental, emotional, and physical life. Examples of possible demonic activity are as follows:

- Fear
- Depression
- Feelings of condemnation
- Despondency, despair, hopelessness
- Fear of the unpardonable sin
- Thoughts of suicide
- Uncontrollable anger and rage
- Masochistic or sadistic behaviors or fantasies
- Escape and withdrawal
- Excessive feelings of loneliness
- Confusion
- Feeling evil or believing that you appear evil to others

> *Evidences of demonization are broad and cover almost every area of a person's mental, emotional, and physical life.*

- Physical infirmities
- Uncontrolled sexual urges (e.g., a desire for pornography)
- Obsessive thoughts and behavior
- Inability to receive affection
- Inability to praise and worship God
- Inability to understand or read the Bible

Obviously, all of us encounter some of these problems at times in our lives, and we shouldn't automatically assume we are oppressed by demons. However, should you have any of these manifestations or signs at a continuing or compulsive level, demonic activity should be considered.

If your problems are mild, you may be able to deal with the demons yourself, without assistance. However, if the problems are more severe and handicapping, you may need help from another believer. Every example of deliverance found in the Bible required a second party to cast the demons out. You, too, may need that kind of help.

The Four Major Hindrances Of Deliverance

According to Romans 14:11, every knee will bow to the name of Jesus Christ. However, we have had some occasions where deliverance didn't work. Obviously, the authority of Christ is perfect, but on the human side there are certain conditions that prohibit progress when dealing with demonic activity in people's lives.

The first major hindrance to deliverance from demons is unforgiveness. According to Matthew 18, unforgiveness releases "tormentors"—demonic spirits who use unforgiveness as an open door and nesting ground for activity. Since unforgiveness releases the tormentors, it is counterproductive to address spirits who have a right to be present. Until unforgiveness is dealt with, progress won't be possible.

The second hindrance to deliverance is the human will. Some people say with their mouths they want help, but really don't. If an individual doesn't want the intruders evicted, they will stay. You can't cast out your friends. You must want the demons to leave. The human will is a powerful thing. When we turn our wills toward God, renouncing the devil and refusing to host his presence in our lives, God will honor our wills and work with us by His Spirit evicting evil spirits and their effects on us.

The third hindrance to deliverance is fear. Some people come to us so fearful of the experience that they block and resist the very thing they want and need. Others are fearful of exposure. They feel sure the Holy Spirit is going to lay out for public scrutiny every sinful or despicable thing they have ever done, and they will be subjected to public humiliation. The Holy Spirit will not address any issue a person is unwilling to examine. Again, God honors an individual's will and operates in an atmosphere of love and gentleness.

Hidden sin is the fourth hindrance to deliverance. Hidden sin is unrepentant sin which will block the power of the Holy Spirit as He ministers freedom to those who are demonically bound. The Spirit of God only works in an atmosphere of truth and purity.

My husband and I ministered to a man who obviously needed help. His marriage was threatened; his boss was going to fire him; and financial ruin was crouching at the door. About fifteen minutes into the session, it became apparent we were getting nowhere. We had reached a block and nothing was happening. He insisted that he was open to ministry and his will was involved in the process. We adjourned for the evening and rescheduled at a later time.

We encountered the same block again and again, achieving no success. As time went on, the Holy Spirit revealed to us that he had a hidden sin. At the next meeting, we told him of the word we believed the Lord had given us and challenged him to reveal anything he might be hiding from us that would hinder God's ministry to him. He then confessed to drug addiction. He was a prescription drug addict and wanted no one to know of his habit. As long as he protected that sin, all deliverance was blocked. However, once it was subjected to the light and he repented, deliverance took place quickly.

Another example of hidden sin was the man who was involved in pornography. He was ashamed and wanted no one to know. He, too, achieved freedom once the hidden sin was exposed.

Unrepentant abortion is another example of hidden sin that blocks deliverance. God takes seriously the shedding of innocent blood. Cain, who premeditatedly killed his brother, suffered exile for the remainder of his life. God told him that the blood of his brother cried out from the ground. Abortion is the shedding of innocent blood and must be recognized as murder and repented of before deliverance can proceed. Even though abortion is a serious sin, God will forgive the guilty parties when they repent. This forgiveness is total and restores those who repent into a fully righteous position before God.

Still another example of hidden sin is unrepentant witchcraft. Many people have dabbled in witchcraft unknowingly. They went to carnival fortune tellers or read horoscopes in the newspaper. As innocent as all of that appears, it is still witchcraft. Any indulgence in witchcraft blocks the ministry of deliverance. It is wise to check for witchcraft prior to any ministry. The enemy is in his territory and will not move unless a person has a sincere, repentant heart.

The Authority of the Name of Jesus

No one personally has any authority over the enemy. All au-

> *Jesus clearly says that we will do greater works than He did, including having authority over all the powers of the enemy, Satan.*

thority over Satan and his kingdom belongs to Jesus. Before His death, He gave authority in His name over all the power of the enemy to those who believed in Him and followed Him (Luke 10:17-20). When He died, Ephesians 4:8 says, *"He ascended on high, He led captivity captive."* Ephesians 4:9 goes on to say *"...that He also first descended into the lower parts of the earth."* On the cross, Jesus conquered Satan and delegated His authority to us. John 14:12-14 says: *"Most assuredly, I say to you, he who believes in Me, the works that I do he will do also; and greater works than these he will do, because I go to My Father. And whatever you ask in My name, that I will do, that the Father may be glorified in the Son. If you ask anything in My name, I will do it"* (NKJV).

Jesus clearly says that we will do greater works than He did, including having authority over all the powers of the enemy, Satan. However, there are two conditions—we have to be believers, and we must use the name of Jesus.

Philippians 2:9-11 says: *"Therefore God also has highly exalted Him and given Him the name which is above every name, that at the name of Jesus every knee should bow, of those in heaven, and of those on earth, and of those under the earth, and that every tongue should confess that Jesus Christ is Lord to the glory of God the Father"* (NKJV).

Every knee must bow to the name of Jesus. Every knee in heaven or on earth or under the earth, whether human or spirit, must yield to the name of Jesus. Jesus' name carries all authority and all power. His name enables us to take authority over demonic force.

To help you understand how this dynamic works, imagine that you are detained at an intersection. Barreling down the road is an eighteen wheeler. This truck weighs more than ten tons and is powered by a diesel engine. Standing in an intersection is a man in a uniform commanding that truck to stop. This trucker wisely heeds the instructions and brakes to a halt. Why does he do this? He is certainly bigger and more powerful than that lone figure positioned in the road. The trucker doesn't personally know the man stopping traffic. However, what the trucker does recognize is a badge on the man's shirt that signifies he is an officer of the state. The trucker doesn't obey the man; he obeys the man's badge and the authority it represents. He knows that all the authority of the state stands behind that badge. If the officer takes his badge off or quits his job, the trucker would no longer be obligated to obey him.

The same principle applies to the spiritual realm. Satan and his host do not obey us personally; they obey the authority of the name of Jesus. Jesus has deputized us to do His work, and in His name we have authority over all the power of the enemy. A word of warning: Don't duplicate the mistake of the seven sons of Sceva as recorded in the nineteenth chapter of the Book of Acts. Though they did invoke the name of Jesus to try to cast out demons, they didn't have a personal knowledge and relationship with the Lord.

Using the name of Jesus and Christian commands to try to cast out demons is unwise if we aren't in right relationship with the Lord. However, if we are in a right relationship with the Lord, we have the authority to boldly command demons and to expect them to obey us. A right relationship with the Lord is established and maintained as we confess our sins honestly and receive the forgiveness He offers by the blood of Jesus. We then walk with God, communing with Him through prayer and His Word. Fellowship with other believers is also important in remaining close to the Lord and receiving the ministry He offers through His Body—the Church.

Even though deliverance is a very important issue, it is only a part of the total picture. It's not a cure-all designed to alleviate all of the problems in your life. Many people come to me wanting me to deliver them from all of their difficulties. Like the physician, they expect me to give them a prescription that will resolve all issues in their lives. Deliverance simply doesn't achieve this end. Deliverance is like arm wrestling. In arm wrestling, contestants place their elbows on a table, with their arms in an upright position. Their hands are firmly clasped. At the signal, they attempt to pin each other's hand to the table. Whoever achieves it first wins.

Our war against sin is similar to arm wrestling. Sin is our opponent and our goal is to overcome its power in our lives. Most people start in the upright position and push against the force by the power of their will. However, if you are affected by demons, you begin with the back of your hand pinned to the table. Before you can even begin to win, you must first battle your way back to the starting position. You arrive at the starting position after you have defeated the power of the demonic in your life, not by the power of your will, but by the power of God.

Deliverance doesn't guarantee success in any given area; it only assures you an even chance of success. You still must overcome the power of sin in your life as you also learn to incorporate essential Christian disciplines into your daily routine. In short, deliverance doesn't assure freedom and healing. Instead it provides you with the opportunity to be free. Once demonic powers are broken, you have established an atmosphere where your will can choose to do what is right without being battered by the enemy.

If you suspect you have some demonic influence in your life, offer a prayer similar to the following: "In the name of Jesus and by the blood of Jesus, I bind a spirit of _____ (the name of the spirit. You can tell the name of a spirit by its nature. A spirit of anger exhibits anger. The same is true with lust, fear, etc.). I command you to leave by the authority of Jesus Christ." Continue to give this command, or one like it, until you believe you have achieved success. Also, quoting Scripture is powerful to overcome demons. For example, if a spirit of fear has been bound, you might say, "Jesus didn't give us a spirit of fear, but of love, power and a sound mind" (II Timothy 1:7).

If your problems are more serious, I suggest you find an appropriate individual to pray and stand with you . Deliverance is a valid and necessary ministry which is especially important to anyone who genuinely desires to be free from his past. Ask the Holy Spirit to reveal to you any areas of your life that could be affected by demons. Also, chapter twenty-one will be helpful to you in learning how to do daily battle with the unseen powers of the enemy.

Freedom From the Fruits of Your Past

Understanding and Overcoming the Present Problems in Your Life which Began and Feed from Your Past

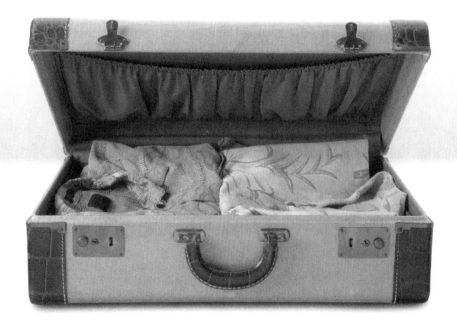

The Fruit of a Distorted Image of God

Chapter 10 Jimmy Evans

God has designed the world in a wonderful way. Specifically, in the way God has designed humans, He has insured that every child born into the world must be the product of a man and woman. God's design for families is that a loving mother and father raise a child in a godly environment throughout his childhood and adolescence.

The importance of parents in the development of a child cannot be overstated. In many ways, parents are to a child what God is to an adult. They are to be the protectors, providers, and nurturers of the child. When the parents accept and fulfill this God-given role, not only does the child grow up in a safe and secure environment, but also, when he is older, he will have a clearer concept of the character of God. Rarely have I seen a child or an adult who didn't relate to God based on his relationship with his parents. If our parents were godly and loving people, we are at an advantage in our ability to relate to God in an intimate, trusting relationship.

However, if we had bad experiences with our parents while growing up, those experiences can taint our concept of God. In trying to help people in counseling, one of the greatest obstacles that must be overcome is an inaccurate and distorted concept of God frequently based on their background and their parents' behavior. Without a proper concept of God, true freedom cannot be achieved or maintained. Therefore, the process of correcting their misconceptions about God based on their pasts is a major step in being set free and finding the future God has for them.

To help you understand how your concept of God may have been clouded or twisted because of your childhood experiences, here are some of the most common misconceptions about God and how one's parents' behavior was a direct influence on shaping those perceptions:

Behavior of Parent	Misconception about God
Legalistic / harsh disciplinarian	God is mad / authoritarian / impersonal / demanding
Perfectionist / extremely high goals / little praise or affirmation	God is never satisfied / always disappointed and upset with me
Little or no affection	God is impersonal, distant
Critical / verbally abusive	God is angry / He puts up with people but doesn't really love them

Behavior of Parent	Misconception about God
Workaholic / focus away from children and outside of the home	God is detached and uncaring / it is difficult to get God's attention / I'm really not that important to Him
Abusive / dominating	God rules by fear / even though I may have to obey Him, I don't really trust Him
Moody / temperamental	God is unpredictable / one day He loves me, the next day He is angry and threatening
Sinful / immoral / low standard of discipline and behavior	God doesn't mean what He says / God is extremely gracious and is a pushover / no need to fear Him
Smothering / doting / spoiling you and never saying no	God exists for me / the only thing that matters is my world / God must conform to my needs and desires
Had favorite children / compared you with siblings and others	God has favorites / He loves "good people" more than sinners / He loves me based on my performance
Made promises and broke them / gave warnings and didn't follow through	God is unreliable and unfaithful / difficult to believe in His Word
Were hypocritical / lived one way at home and another way in public	God isn't powerful or relevant / religion is for social and special purposes / doesn't relate to my life

Though there are exceptions to the rule, most people's concept of God is greatly influenced by their parents' behaviors. As you can see from the list comparing parents' behavior to our concept of God, there is a direct parallel between how we viewed our parents and how we view God. This parallel is a critical point in being freed from the incorrect perspectives we have of God. Once we understand the parallel between our parents and God, we can then begin to make progress toward finding a true, biblical concept of God.

The process of healing our misconceptions really starts when we realize that our parents' behavior doesn't dictate or demonstrate God's nature. Though parents are important in our lives, they are imperfect and mortal. This isn't true of God. He is perfect and immortal. When we attempt to understand the nature and character of God by using human standards, we are making a big mistake that has eternal consequences.

God wants parents, pastors, other adults, and political leaders to be righteous role models to children; however, the sad fact remains that it rarely happens the way God desires. Consequently, people in important authority positions miscommunicate to children the true nature of godly authority. The degree to which we mismodel the nature of God is the same degree to which they will struggle to understand God. Unfortunately, many children can't see past the failures of their parents and authority figures to understand the character of God. Rather, the children simply accept their parents' and leaders' behavior as the final demonstration of who God is.

On our journey to finding freedom from our past, we must separate God's character from the failures of people. To attribute to God every imperfection and sin of our parents is a terrible mistake. Even though many of us do it unconsciously, we must honestly evaluate our concept of God and truthfully admit if our perspective of God has been changed or distorted by human failures. Once we are truthful about this issue and are willing to separate human performance from divine character, we have made an important step forward.

Once we realize how our parents failed to accurately present God's love and character to us, we must admit that they were wrong and forgive them. Covering for our parents or making apologies for them is counter-productive. On the other hand, holding grudges against our parents for their mistakes is also wrong. The only way to find freedom is to see our parents as they are and to forgive them.

Let's assume your parents were critical and verbally abusive. Your first step would be to recognize that the criticism and abuse is contrary to God's character. During this process, it is important to identify your parents' behaviors as harsh and unbiblical. Once you have come to terms with those two issues, you can then forgive them for their sins, inadequacies, mistakes, or abuses. As you release your parents from your judgment and unforgiveness, you will be free to discover the true nature of God without any deceptions or distortions blocking your way.

Once you have forgiven your parents or others who may have harmed your concept of God when you were a child, the next step is to ask the Holy Spirit to teach you the truth about God. Before ascending from the earth to sit at the right hand of God the Father, Jesus said to His

> *Once we realize how our parents failed to accurately present God's love and character to us, we must admit that they were wrong and forgive them.*

> *When we ask the Holy Spirit to teach us about God, we need to be aware that the chief means He uses to teach us is the Word of God.*

disciples: *"However, when He, the Spirit of truth, has come, He will guide you into all truth; for He will not speak on His own authority, but whatever He hears He will speak; and He will tell you things to come. He will glorify Me, for He will take of what is Mine and declare it to you. All things that the Father has are Mine. Therefore I said that He will take of Mine and declare it to you"* (John 16:13-15, NKJV).

The best way for any of us to learn about God is to be taught by God Himself. The Holy Spirit is God. He has been sent as the third Person of the Godhead to minister truth to us. He takes from the things of God and personally ministers them to the submitted heart and mind. As we seek to learn about God, we need the leadership and ministry of the Holy Spirit. Jesus said, *"He will guide you into all truth…"* It is impossible for the Holy Spirit to lie or distort the truth. As we ask Him to lead us daily, His enlightenment will reveal the true nature of God. The result is transforming.

When we ask the Holy Spirit to teach us about God, we need to be aware that the chief means He uses to teach us is the Word of God. Even though the Holy Spirit will on many occasions speak directly to our hearts and minds, He relies heavily on the Scriptures to teach us about God. The Bible is full of examples of God's nature. If we ask the Holy Spirit to interpret the Bible to us, He will guide us into a full and balanced understanding of what the Bible has to say about God and many other subjects. The Holy Spirit is the author of the Bible and, as such, is the only one truly qualified to lead us to a full understanding of it.

If we submit our minds to the Holy Spirit and to the Word of God, we can be healed of every impediment that hinders a correct understanding of God. One of the greatest challenges for someone with a distorted image of God is to learn to think of Him in new ways. The only way this can take place is for us to do the following: Admit that we've been wrong to limit our understanding of God to our experience with humans; forgive our parents and others who have mismodeled God's nature to us; ask the Holy Spirit to teach us the true nature of God as we submit to His voice and the voice of Scripture; and believe what God's Word and the Holy Spirit reveal to us, even if it is different from what we have previously thought. By faith, act as though it is true, even if our emotions or memories tell us differently.

Seven Attributes of the Nature of God

Seven attributes of God make up His basic nature. Though it is impossible for us to totally comprehend or define God in this life, we can know His general attributes by what His Word says about Him. These seven attributes are all important, eternal parts of God's nature. These elements are always active and true for every person in every generation.

1. God is holy.

> *"Exalt the LORD our God, and worship at His holy hill; for the lord our God is holy"* (Psalm 99:9, NKJV).

The word holy means "separated from sin." According to many accounts in the Bible, we understand that God has no part in sin and is Himself perfect and unchangeable.

2. God is loving and compassionate.

"Beloved, let us love one another, for love is of God; and everyone who loves is born of God and knows God. He who does not love does not know God, for God is love" (1 John 4:7-8, NKJV).

"The LORD is gracious and full of compassion, slow to anger and great in mercy. The lord is good to all, and His tender mercies are over all His works" (Psalm 145:8-9, NKJV).

"And Jesus, when He came out, saw a great multitude and was moved with compassion for them, because they were like sheep not having a shepherd. So He began to teach them many things" (Mark 6:34, NKJV).

"Indeed we count them blessed who endure. You have heard of the perseverance of Job and seen the end intended by the Lord—that the Lord is very compassionate and merciful" (James 5:11, NKJV).

Some people think that just because God is holy, He is also uncaring and legalistic. That is untrue. God is holy, but He is also brokenhearted over the suffering of people. His tender, compassionate heart motivates His saving grace and constant mercies to be directed toward us. His love is greater than any mother, father, wife, or husband who has ever lived. He is loyal, gracious, merciful, and long-suffering. God has a capacity to forgive and forget our faults more than any human ever could.

3. God is unchangeable.

"Jesus Christ is the same yesterday, today, and forever" (Hebrews 13:8, NKJV).

"For I am the LORD, *I do not change"* (Malachi 3:6a, NKJV).

The same God who loved us so much that He sent His Son to die for us still loves us as much today. His holiness, truth, character, and nature are unchangeable. God is not unstable or moody. Rather, God is the most stable personality in the universe. He will never be corrupted. His love never changes. His commitment to us never changes. Once we understand this, we will have greater security within.

4. God is omnipotent.

"And I heard, as it were, the voice of a great multitude, as the sound of many waters and as the sound of mighty thunderings, saying, 'Alleluia! For the Lord God Omnipotent reigns!'" (Revelation 19:6, NKJV).

"But Jesus looked at them and said to them, 'With men this is impossible, but with God all things are possible'" (Matthew 19:26, NKJV).

We never have reason to feel hopeless about a problem or circumstance we are facing. God has all power and is able to set us free and to give us the supernatural ability to live above our circumstances. God has power over the devil, sin, man, and nature. There is nothing He cannot do.

5. God is omnipresent.

"Where can I go from Your Spirit? Or where can I flee from Your presence? If I ascend into heaven, You are there; if I make my bed in hell, behold, You are there. If I take the wings of the morning, and dwell in the uttermost parts of the sea, even there Your hand shall lead me, and Your right hand shall hold me. If I say, 'Surely the darkness shall fall

on me,' even the night shall be light about me; indeed, the darkness shall not hide from You, but the night shines as the day; the darkness and the light are both alike to You" (Psalm 139:7-12, NKJV).

"'Behold, the virgin shall be with child, and bear a Son, and they shall call His name Immanuel,' which is translated, 'God with us'" (Matthew 1:23, NKJV).

You can never be any place in your life where God isn't with you. He has been with you since the day you were conceived in your mother's womb. His presence is an intimate, personal presence designed to draw you into a close, personal relationship with Him. As you understand His presence with you and begin to acknowledge it, it will change your concept of God from a distant Being somewhere in heaven to a personal God walking with you through every valley and mountaintop in life.

6. God is omniscient.

"For if our heart condemns us, God is greater than our heart, and knows all things" (1 John 3:20, NKJV).

There isn't any area of knowledge, reality, or truth that God doesn't know and fully understand. God knows the reason He created us in our mothers' wombs. He knows every hurt and fear hidden inside of our hearts. He knows every sin of our past and pres-

> *When we grasp the fact that God knows all things, it should produce in us a willingness to trust His leadership and authority.*

ent. He also knows the hidden sins of our lives that no one else is aware of. God also knows the future of each one of us and the path each of us should take for victory and success. When we grasp the fact that God knows all things, it should produce in us a willingness to trust His leadership and authority. God knows everything about us, good and bad, and still loves us deeply and wants a relationship with us. This is the measure of true love.

7. God is faithful.

"God is faithful, by whom you were called into the fellow-ship of His Son, Jesus Christ our Lord" (1 Corinthians 1:9, NKJV).

"Your faithfulness endures to all generations; You estab-lished the earth, and it abides" (Psalm 119:90, NKJV).

When God makes a covenant or a promise, it is impossible for Him to break that promise. When God begins a work in our lives, He is faithful to continue that work, even when we fail. He is faithful to forgive us when we confess our sins. He is faithful to answer prayers, as we put our faith in Him. He is faithful to provide for us and lead us, as we look to Him as our Shepherd and Provider. We never need to worry about the faithfulness of God. He is the most faithful friend we will ever have.

I hope something you've read in this chapter will help you to see a bigger and greater God than you've been able to see before. With such an incredible God reaching out to us, to love us and care for us eternally, it would be a tragedy for any of us to miss what He has in store because of our inability or unwillingness to look beyond the people of our past. In order for us to be set free from the failures of people in our lives and to truly understand God, we must learn to separate human behavior from God's character. People need our love, grace, and forgiveness. God deserves our worship and adoration. He is an awesome God!

The Fruit of Shame:

A Distorted Self-Image

Chapter 11 Ann Billington

Are you motivated by guilt? Do you find yourself apologizing even when you are right? Does it seem that every time there is a conflict in a relationship, it is always your fault? Are you easily manipulated and controlled? Perhaps you feel defective, incomplete, or abnormal. When you compare yourself with others, do you always feel you hold the short end of the stick? Does it seem that when God created you, He left out some vital and important parts, leaving you incomplete to function and survive the best you could? If you can identify with these thoughts and attitudes, you may be dealing with issues related to shame. Because shame is frequently confused with guilt, condemnation, conviction, and inferiority, it is important that we differentiate between these terms.

Guilt is a response to something you have done; it is a reaction to your behavior. Perhaps you have sinned, committed an offense, or violated a relationship, and you deeply regret your action. These situations usually generate guilt, which leads to one of two responses—condemnation or conviction. If guilt becomes unhealthy, it develops into feelings of condemnation. Condemnation is an overall sense of failure and sinfulness that offers no clear way of penance to be reconciled to God or man. According to Romans 8:1, there is no condemnation in Jesus. Therefore, condemnation, though common, must be rejected as unhealthy and unbiblical.

The opposite of condemnation is conviction. Conviction is a healthy response to guilt. Conviction is our impetus for change, allowing the Holy Spirit to transform us into the image of Jesus. Conviction is a clear sense of guilt accompanied with a specific solution. It produces a state of mind that brings repentance and a change of behavior. The author of conviction is the Holy Spirit. John 16:8-11 says, *"And when He has come, He will convict the world of sin, and of righteousness, and of judgment: of sin, because they do not believe in Me; of righteousness, because I go to My Father and you see Me no more; of judgment, because the ruler of this world is judged"* (NKJV). So, our response to sin or wrongdoing is guilt. Guilt will then evolve into either unhealthy condemnation or the healthy conviction of the Holy Spirit. The first produces torment, while the latter produces repentance and release.

Shame, though frequently confused with guilt, condemnation, and conviction, is different. Unlike guilt, shame is not a response to something you have done, but a response to who and what you perceive yourself to be. You, yourself, are not quite right, not normal, not okay. You believe the very essence of who you are is defective. It's not that you have *done* anything wrong or bad; it's that you *are* wrong and bad. Guilt, condemnation, and conviction are feelings caused by sin or something one has done; shame is an assessment of one's very being.

You might ask, "What is the difference between shame and deep feelings of inferiority?" Feelings of inferiority arise when we compare ourselves with others. Using as standards those desirable traits or qualities we see in others, we believe them to be absent or inferior in ourselves. Comparison is a sin, which produces negative results. Only two things can follow this line of thinking. Both are bad and set us up for failure. We will either look good in our own eyes, which leads to pride, or we will look inadequate, releasing feelings of inferiority.

Shame is different. It is not merely a comparison, but rather, it is a verdict of self-hate rendered by a judge and jury of one. Shame is actually the energy behind feelings of inferiority, which entice us to compare ourselves with others. Shame is an inner sensing of defectiveness that colors our emotions and relationships and drives us toward self-deprecating behavior.

A preteen girl who had been sexually abused as a young child related to me the feelings she had about her body. Her body repulsed her. She felt her body was dirty. She would look at her legs or arms and actually detest them. This twelve-year-old girl became sexually active and took drugs for the first time the year she was abused in an effort to allay the torturous feelings of shame. She ran away from home and began living on the streets. One evening three young men brought her into our drug abuse clinic. The previous night had

> *Shame is an inner sensing of defectiveness that colors our emotions and relationships and drives us toward self-deprecating behavior.*

been spent in a motel room with six men. Stoned and frightened, she sought refuge with us. Yet, when given an opportunity to escape her circumstances, she refused. In her mind, she deserved the treatment she received. Shame consumed this girl, producing self-hate and self-destructive behavior. Like unforgiveness, shame is a cancer that consumes and destroys its host.

Shame comes to us in a variety of ways, but nearly all paths to shame involve some loss, perceived loss, or trauma that generates pain. At times it appears that people will go to almost any length to avoid hurt, but all pain and loss must be grieved. Shame must be faced, dealt with, and put behind us. There is no way around those uncomfortable feelings.

Most people fear pain so much that they use unhealthy ways to deal with it. In order to avoid pain, they resort to denial, where they rationalize or outright refuse to acknowledge pain. Denial is a form of self-deception that allows them to believe a lie, thus circumventing God's natural grieving process. The abused twelve-year-old's deception was a form of denial that blocked pain and truth. She didn't view herself as a victim, but rather viewed herself as the guilty party.

Because she failed to tell her mother about her stepfather's clandestine visits to her room, she assumed responsibility for an act that was, in fact, a heinous violation of her. She believed she was a bad person; she must have wanted sex. In her thinking there must have been something in her that attracted him. She was defective or he would not have come to her room. Failing to tell her mother only further entombed her shame, locking up the pain in her heart. The reality of how bad she was overwhelmed her. She compared herself to all the "normal" people and became convinced that she was different. Not only did the abused girl take responsibility for her stepfather's sin, but in the process assessed herself as defective.

Rather than understanding the truth, this girl believed a lie and her life was forever changed by her self-deception. To avoid the pain, it became more palatable to condemn and punish herself for existing. Jesus says, *"And you shall know the truth and the truth shall make you free"* (John 8:32, NKJV). The truth was that she was not guilty. The act that so shamed and degraded her was not her fault. There was nothing in her that sexually attracted her stepfather, but rather she was victimized by her stepfather's sin. This loss of innocence and trust needed to be grieved and released. Denial only complicated and delayed the grieving and healing process.

By denying truth, shame-bound people also deny their emotions. They refuse to feel. With their refusal to acknowledge pain also comes a determination to avoid it. There are some who think they can be selective about the feelings they choose to feel and those they choose to reject. They believe they can turn feelings off and on as they wish. However, the truth is that once they start denying one emotion, they begin a process that turns off all emotions, both good and bad. They can't keep all the pleasant feelings and reject only the unpleasant ones. This tendency to reject feelings only deepens the denial and deception.

Once denial of truth and feelings is birthed, shame-bound people are now open for a wide array of defensive behaviors. They will go to great lengths to avoid and alleviate the feelings of shame. An example is obsessive performance. This is a defensive behavior that is motivated largely by a fear of failure.

Recently a well-dressed, professional-looking woman entered my office armed with a time management system in one hand and a clipboard in the other. She was prepared to attack her problems with the same energy and efficiency she used to approach her real estate business. This highly successful woman seemed to thrive on pressure and activity. However, underneath the veneer of efficiency was an individual who would soon buckle under the strain of performance. She, too, was a shame-bound person who was using her achievements to alleviate her deep feelings of defectiveness.

Every challenge became a test of her worth. Failure was unthinkable, unacceptable. Her accomplishments were her identity. With so much on the line, success was imperative. Success became an insatiable monster that demanded more and more food all the time. With every achievement the standards just got greater. Finally, burned out and exhausted, she came to the end of herself. Fear consumed her. Even though she was terrified with thoughts of failing, she was physically, mentally, and emotionally unable to continue. Thoughts of suicide became familiar friends as she slipped deeper and deeper into depression. Because shame was entrenched in her, obsessive performance became her avenue of denying pain and of establishing her worth.

Another behavior related to shame is striving for perfection. The manner by which most people try to maintain perfection is through control. They are compelled to control others, their environment, along with anything and everything that touches their lives. These individuals become very agitated and uneasy when their expectations are not met. Since their goal of perfection is impossible, their lives begin to deteriorate when perfection becomes more and more difficult to achieve.

Control and perfection were problems for a young man who was an attractive, rising executive in a large insurance firm. He was twenty-three years old and impeccably dressed, looking as if he was a model for a fashionable men's clothing line. Initially, he sought help regarding his marriage of two years. As so many times is the case, he married a woman who was his exact opposite. She was by nature very laid-back and easygoing. In contrast, he had been orderly, organized, and efficient all of his life. To make matters worse, they had a new baby boy who disrupted his dad's world in a big way. In addition to his full-time job, this young man was completing his master's degree while working part-time for a printing company.

Since perfection was the only acceptable standard in every arena of his life, anything less than perfection was loathsome. So, between a new marriage, graduate school, a new baby and a full-time job, perfection became the impossible dream. As his ability to perform to his standards deteriorated, his personality began to change. He became impatient, insufferable, and hostile. A perfect house was simply not an important goal for his young wife. When her perfectionist husband returned home, he would fly into a rage at any disorder he encountered. He was usually up in the mornings at 5:00 a.m. to study. By 9:00 a.m., he was hard at work. Then, at night he either called on potential clients or was attending night classes.

One particular evening after failing a mid-term exam he returned to a house that didn't meet his standards. He lost control and exploded in a rage that frightened his wife. Over the next several weeks, his wife worked harder and harder to meet his expectations. He was never satisfied. He became increasingly irritable as he lost control over his life and his standard of perfection began to slip. Finally, their relationship was jeopardized.

Obviously, this young man was bound by his needs for

both perfection and success. Over the years he had developed patterns of perfection to alleviate the shame caused by a doting, smothering mother who had emotionally replaced her husband with her son. It was, in a sense, a form of emotional incest. Now, his world was falling apart. He could no longer satisfy the insatiable monster of perfection. Like the performance-oriented woman realtor, he was using perfection as a weapon to subdue the shadows of shame that followed him all of his life.

Many performance-oriented, perfectionist parents impose feelings of shame onto their children by putting impossible expectations on them. Their children must act right, look right, be right; anything less is unsatisfactory. Because the children are viewed as extensions of the parents, the children's performance and failures become a personal issue with the parents. Frequently, the parents' and the children's identities become one. Consequently, the parents' shame becomes a factor if their children fail.

Recently at a basketball game, a father became irate at his child's performance. Since he was the coach, he pulled his eight-year-old son from the court and began to verbally assault him. One would have thought we were attending the NBA playoffs instead of a local neighborhood league game. The child was berated for every mistake. Only perfection was acceptable; anything less reflected badly on the parent. The ugly scene made me wonder, "Who was really on the court, the father or the son?" Perfection was the way this parent continued to deny his shame. But worse, he was now creating shame in his son.

Two more conditions related to performance and perfection are anorexia and bulimia. Both are serious eating disorders. Not only do these conditions stem from performance and control, but also they are very much connected with a deep sense of shame and a distorted self-image. These conditions appear to be more prevalent in women than men, with the onset most frequently occurring between the ages of thirteen and twenty-five.

Anorexia is by far the more serious of the two disorders, as a person can literally starve herself to death. A bulimic indulges in a binge-purge cycle in which the victim binges on food and then vomits it up or uses laxatives to further purge her body. Unlike anorexics, bulimics can sometimes appear normal and maintain an average body weight. Anorexics can also be bulimic. They might starve themselves, eating practically nothing, as they also exercise obsessively. Occasionally, they will binge, losing control and eating voraciously. Then, with guilt and remorse they look at their distended stomachs and resort to bulimic patterns to purge.

Anorexia and bulimia are complex problems. Within the last decade, much attention has been given to these eating disorders. Since the death of the singer Karen Carpenter, greater concern has developed for those victimized by these problems. However, there is still much speculation as to what causes anorexia and bulimia and why it seems to be increasing. Because of the life-threatening potential of these problems, a physician should closely supervise a person suffering from them.

However, it becomes clear as we talk with individuals who have eating disorders that they are often dealing with a deep sense of shame. Control, performance, and perfection become key instruments for them to manage a fragile self-identity. Obviously those suffering with eating disorders have also bought Satan's lie peddled by the media that thin is beautiful, and they have attempted to conform to that image. Young women who have confessed to eating disorders believe their success and security are bound up in their bodies. Some have reported that they felt that their lives were out of control, and their sense of control returned whenever they controlled their food consumption.

Again, the obsessive nature of anorexia lends credence to the presence of demons. However, a word of caution—we must not be so naive as to think deliverance will in and of itself cure eating disorders. Far more is involved and all issues must be addressed as well. People with eating disorders have resorted to starvation and/or purging to try to meet their inner needs and to deal with deep emotional problems. Therefore, careful and complete care must be prayerfully pursued.

Addictions are another avenue shame-bound people use to contend with their pain. Some anesthetize themselves with drugs, while others resort to food, sex, relationships, or alcohol. All of these objects of addiction give the hurting person a feeling of control and peace. With these addictions they can control how they feel and console themselves with a false comfort. With these crutches, the nights are not as dark nor the days too bright. The pain is bearable and the fears dissipate, at least for the moment.

Unfortunately, stark reality re-emerges. Too often, it is too late, for their destructive behavior, like a mad dog, turns on them. Their monster now has two heads, addiction and pain. No longer are they dealing with pain and loss, but now they are also dealing with a full-blown addiction that is controlling their lives. Thoughts of suicide pursue them and, in some cases, snare them irrevocably. Jesus died for such as these. He came to "set the captives free." These unfortunate people are indeed in the grip of "the enemy." They have chosen a method of denial and avoidance of pain that exacts a disastrous price and yields nothing but bondage and more pain.

Some shame-bound individuals use relationships as a method to deny and manage shame. Because they usually come from dysfunctional families, they desperately need love and acceptance, which block feelings of shame. Unfortunately, they usually lack the skills necessary to relate healthily and, therefore, frequently fail. This failure creates even deeper shame. Consequently, they either avoid deep relationships or move from one failed relationship to another, searching for an intimacy that eludes them.

Co-dependency is a relationship problem that has at its core internalized shame. Co-dependents tend to look outside themselves for validation. For example, their intense need for approval causes them to be whatever is required by almost anyone. Many co-dependents have a compulsive need to "fix" and "rescue"—find a wrong and make it right; find a need and meet it; find a hurt, make it better.

> Co-dependents tend to look outside themselves for validation. For example, their intense need for approval causes them to be whatever is required by almost anyone.

Their personal sovereignty and identity don't exist.

To prevent relationship failure and the increased shame it causes, they become whatever they perceive another wants them to be. Their identity enmeshes with those around them, allowing them to further deny shame. They become responsible for the significant people in their lives, instead of leaving that responsibility to God. Shame-bound people have hungry, empty souls that are crying for intimacy. Their greatest need, like all of us, is to be unconditionally loved and accepted. Yet, because of the bondage of their souls, they are unable to drink from the well of healthy relationships. Consequently, every relationship they risk is on a slow road to destruction.

For shame-bound people to heal, they need to develop four behaviors. These behaviors are recognition, determination, thought-life, and forgiveness. Before shame-bound people can halt their destructive journey, they must recognize and admit the inadequacies and pain in their lives. The ability to recognize issues of shame, denial, and their related behaviors must be present. If individuals cannot perceive their problems, they will be impotent to change.

The two sources that fuel denial are pride and fear. A shame-bound person is barely hanging on to his fractured self-image. To admit deficiencies is to further deepen a sense of shame and defectiveness. For example, since shame is at the core of his being, to readily admit to his need for high quality performance or perfection further deepens his feelings of abnormality. He is already performing mental and physical gymnastics to cover his pain and shame. To expose his strategies for managing shame strikes fear in his heart. Therefore, pride will energize his life as he weaves intricate deceptions around himself to shore up an empty identity.

Pride blocks truth. Because of this condition, a shame-bound person often will not recognize destructive patterns or behavior. Also, a shame-bound person is usually defensive when confronted with his problems. This defensive response is a red flag that pride and fear are present. These issues must be overcome before any healing can take place. The answer for pride in a person dealing with shame is to acknowledge the true condition of his heart. Even though it is difficult and painful, healing requires honesty. Along with a confession of truth, the prideful person also must repent for the dishonesty and resistance to God that his pride produced. With repentance and acceptance of truth, the stronghold of pride is broken.

As with pride, fear must be faced or the healing process will be circumvented. Fear of pain and emotional trauma also create unwillingness in individuals to recognize their problems. They have spent a lifetime denying pain and emotion and greatly fear that the self-protective wall they have carefully built will crumble. However, if they refuse to accept pain as a natural part of life and experience it, they will continue their destructive lifestyles. Unfortunately, sometimes people must hit rock bottom before they recognize and admit their problems. They may suffer immeasurable losses, disappointments, and failures. At that low point, though, they may begin to recognize and admit their problems and start to search for answers. This will be the beginning of healing.

Another requirement for healing involves a determination to change. An individual must be committed to repentance and a turning away from destructive thinking and actions. The young man whose marriage was in jeopardy because of his perfectionist, performance-oriented ways must recognize his unhealthy behavior, realize its destructiveness, and make efforts to change. For example, as a person recognizes control and manipulation in his behavior, he must repent, see the detrimental effects, and determine not to use it to achieve his ends. Instead, a person accustomed to implementing control and manipulation must learn to take his hands off of the situation and allow God to be God. By using control and manipulation to achieve his ends, he has played God in his own life and in the lives of others. A commitment to change is paramount to healing.

Isaiah 55:8-9 says that God's thoughts are not our thoughts, and His ways are not our ways. People committed to change must also change the way they think. Their thoughts have not been God's thoughts, but rather the thoughts of their own pain and pride. For true change, we must renew our minds to think God's thoughts. We accomplish this task by dedication to God's Word and a commitment to implement it in our lives. As we read the Bible daily, we learn to gird up the loins of our minds and to take every thought captive. The Scriptures endow our minds with power and revelation as new patterns of thought begin to build us up and change us from the inside.

Also, for there to be any lasting change in your life, you must forgive those who have wronged or abused you. Forgiving for many is a difficult and seemingly impossible task. If you have been abused, it is easy to understand this difficulty. However, the ramifications of unforgiveness may be deadly to you, the wounded person. Sometimes you will experience guilt and condemnation if you are unable to forgive. Allow the Holy Spirit to lead you. As you heal, you will be able to forgive more readily. (If necessary, refer to the chapter on forgiveness in the previous section for more help.)

Lastly, healthy relationships must be established in your life. It is not enough to recognize your problem, to be determined to change, to renew your thought-life, and to forgive. You will

> *It is not enough to recognize your problem, to be determined to change, to renew your thought-life, and to forgive. You will not be truly healed until you risk intimate relationships once again.*

not be truly healed until you risk intimate relationships once again. Usually, shame-bound people believe intimacy is futile. Since intimate relationships are where they experienced pain, abuse, and failure, they tend to erroneously believe intimacy is unacceptable.

Actually, the human soul was created to desire and need intimacy. Consequently, true and lasting healing will not occur until relationships have been successfully achieved. Stepping back into relationships is not unlike mounting a horse after one has been thrown off. Every healing person has to go back into the arena of relationship that created the failure and successfully relate. Sometimes God creates situations where the healing person re-establishes a healthy relationship from an unhealthy relationship from his hurting past. At other times God will bring new, fresh relationships as laboratories for healing. Remember, relationship is very important to God. That includes both one's relationship with Him and with others. There is no such thing as complete healing within a vacuum of isolation. Though God may call you apart into defined, temporary periods of separation, He won't allow that to become a permanent refuge from emotional vulnerability.

Healing takes time. Even though God has it within His power to heal us instantaneously, seldom have I seen Him work this way. He leads us out of the abyss one step at a time. This process of healing, though relatively short, seems an eternity to the hurting person. However, you will reap in due season if you "do not grow weary of well doing." The next chapters explore the problems of relationship abuse. Shame, as we have seen in this chapter, cripples us relationally, making us vulnerable to abusive relationships. We will seek further to understand and get healing from some of the more detailed and intense problems in this area.

The Fruit of Relationship Abuse:

Part I–The Reason for Wrong Relationships

Chapter 12 Ann Billington

Why was I born? What is my purpose on earth? For centuries ancient and modern philosophers pondered these questions as they futilely attempted to explain man's purpose. From the Stoics and Gnostics of the Greek and Roman empires to the eighteenth century existentialist, man has attempted to define his existence apart from God.

In all these centuries little has changed. Today, the secular humanist reduces man to an evolutionary accident with no divine beginning or end. Because the humanist believes man is basically good and all behavior is relative to the cir-

> *To insure that mankind would relate, God created within him three basic needs—love security, and significance.*

cumstances, man's purposes and goals are selfish and self-centered. Therefore, man's desires and self-devotion become the subjective standard for all values.

However, if the Bible is accepted as the explanation for mankind's existence, the reason for birth and purpose in life becomes clear. First, God made man for Himself. Before the fall, Adam and God were in relationship; they walked and talked together in the cool of the day. The Scriptures are replete with man's desire to know God. And, according to Hebrews 8:10-11, God desires for man to know Him. *"For this is the covenant that I will make with the house of Israel: After those days, says the LORD, I will put My laws in their mind and write them on their hearts; and I will be their God, and they shall be My people. None of them shall teach his neighbor, and none his brother, saying, 'Know the LORD,' for all shall know Me, from the least of them to the greatest of them"* (NKJV).

The second purpose for one's life is relationship with others. After God created the world, the animals, and Adam, He judged them as good. The only circumstance in the first two chapters of Genesis that God found lacking was the absence of a companion for Adam. He saw that man was lonely and needed a counterpart. So, He made a woman out of Adam's side, creating the first human relationship. The first two chapters of Genesis establish relationship with God and relationship with one another as the two greatest purposes of man.

Jesus says it another way: *"Thou shalt love the Lord thy God with all thy heart, and with all thy soul, and with all thy mind. This is the first and great commandment. And the second is like unto it, Thou shalt love thy neighbor as thyself. On these two commandments hang all the law and the prophets"* (Matthew 22:37-40, KJV). Man's greatest commandment is to love God with all his heart. The second greatest commandment is to love each other. Again, relationship is the center around which our existence revolves. Man is not an island unto himself, but a social being designed to relate to God and man.

To insure that mankind would relate, God created within him three basic needs—love, security, and significance. Initially, God played a pivotal role in gratifying those needs. He entered an intimate relationship with Adam and Eve, which in itself met their created appetite for love, security, and significance. Adam and Eve's requirement for love was completely satisfied by God, who defined Himself as "love." How insecure or insignificant could Adam be when he walked and talked with the Creator of the universe? So, while Adam and Eve walked in obedience, God met their basic emotional and physical requirements.

God designed these same basic essentials to steer human relationships as well. Adam selflessly met Eve's needs, and Eve selflessly met Adam's needs. Since sin had not polluted the world, selfishness was nonexistent. Adam and Eve lived in an environment where their every desire was completely, joyfully, and healthily met. So complete was the fulfillment of their lives that they probably were unaware of the power of the needs lying within them. However, when Adam and Eve sinned, they rejected God's perfect provision, and their spiritual communion with God ceased. As a result, mankind developed a ravenous hunger for love, security, and significance. They became insatiably "self" focused instead of "other" focused, and turning inward, began striving to meet their own needs by their own means.

At this point, Cain and Abel were not yet born. In God's original plan, the family was the chief resource through which children would learn relationship. God told Adam and Eve to multiply and subdue the earth. He also said that a man should leave his father and mother and cleave to his wife. These statements of purpose created the nucleus around which the family unit would revolve. Clearly, children were to be brought into a family where their emotional and physical needs would be met by God and their parents.

Unfortunately, children didn't appear until after the fall (Genesis 4). Decay and perversion were already in process. Mankind was alienated from God's perfect provision, and today we are still groping for ways in which to satisfy our needs. When God rejected Cain's sacrifice, Cain's need for significance and love was threatened. In his anger, murder infiltrated his heart. Genesis 4:7 records God's urgent plea to master the sin that was lying at the door. God affirmed Cain by telling him that he would be accepted if he resisted the sin. Here, we have the first example of man attempting to meet his own needs with his own hands. Since then, world history has become little more than a chronicle of mankind's futile efforts to gratify his own needs apart from God. As fallen man degenerated in his lust to satisfy himself, God eventually regretted that He ever made him. Therefore, He destroyed the entire earth and all its inhabitants, saving only Noah and his family.

However, God did not give up on man. He developed a redemptive plan, which included the nation of Israel and the Messiah. Because of man's selfish, depraved nature, God explicitly spelled out the standards of relationship. For the Israelites, the Ten Commandments dictated the order of relationship with God and man. After the Ten Commandments,

Jesus came personally to explain to us the method by which we could love God and each other as God intended.

With Jesus, man once again can look to God to personally meet his needs of love, security, and significance. Parents, armed with the insight and power of the Holy Spirit, can raise children to love and be loved by God. Christian families once again can become the classrooms through which children will learn right relationship with God and man.

Unfortunately, we still live in a fallen world inhabited by Satan and his demons. As Christians, our lives vastly improve, but we are by no means walking in a paradise. Though redeemed, mankind still has a flesh nature that is selfish and must be countered by obedience to the Word and the empowerment of the Holy Spirit. In short, man runs into problems when he attempts to meet his needs of love, security, and significance by his own efforts apart from God. These attempts inevitably lead to serious relationship problems rooted in selfishness and self-devotion.

With selfishness and self-devotion at the root of man's nature, difficulties arise as he attempts to meet his three basic needs. For example, the human's need for love transcends time, race, and nationality. The orphaned child in Bosnia yearns for parental love as much as the affluent American teenager. Isaac, Abraham's son, was no exception. Genesis 24:67 reveals that Isaac was not comforted after the death of his mother until he married his wife, Rebekah. His heart ached for the love of his mother and grief filled his soul. After his marriage to Rebekah, Isaac seemingly went on with his life, raising a family through which God would fulfill His covenant with man.

Love is one of our most basic needs. When left unmet, it can produce a hunger for approval and a fear of rejection that can cripple or destroy a person's life. People who have been starved for love might become promiscuous, dependent, or compliant. An individual's need for love is like his physical need for food and water. He can't survive without it and will resort to an assortment of desperate behaviors to satisfy it.

Man's attempt to satisfy his need for security apart from God also produces its share of trouble. Since the time Adam was told he would have to sweat a living out of the land, man has fearfully endeavored to establish and maintain a secure life. One can only imagine Adam's feelings when he lost the safety of the garden and surveyed a hostile world. When the basic need of security is unmet, fear can become a major problem, creating the potential for control and manipulation, aggressiveness, or compliance.

Confusion is another byproduct of insecurity. How baffling life must have become for Adam as he tried to make sense of a world gone awry. Never before did Adam have to assess a perplexing world and determine how he would live. Now, like the rich man in Luke 12:16-20, mankind searches for ways to build bigger barns to store up security and bring peace to the uncertainty of life. In similar fashion, many people place their security in money, savings accounts, and investments, never feeling they have enough. Though money is an obvious first choice as a method to achieve security, interestingly, man doesn't always place his security in tangibles. Sometimes, he draws security from relationships instead. This situation can yield co-dependency or produce serious abandonment issues. In fact, it is easy to become dependent on anything or anyone that provides security. Security, like love, is a very important need, motivating people in their jobs and relationships. However, the need for security, like the need for love, can produce a host of problem issues in an individual's life, if this need is satisfied apart from God.

Unlike animals, mankind has a desire for significance. Adam and Eve lost a privileged position of eminence when they sinned. They were intimate with *Elohim*, the great and awesome God, and the Creator of the universe. They walked and talked with Jehovah. Once outside the garden, that place in their hearts was empty; that privileged position was gone.

Adam and Eve, along with the rest of mankind, turned inward to themselves to guarantee significance. This need to feel significant is still within man and, if unmet, produces many problems such as poor self-esteem and distorted self-image. Children who suffer rejection may spend their lives attempting to feel important, or perhaps they become like the prostitute who masochistically subjects herself to endless degradation, which reinforces the image of worthlessness resident in her soul.

Mankind desperately needs to feel important and special. A man who gunned down four people was asked why he did it. He said, "I wanted to be somebody." Gang members, when asked why they were involved in gangs, stated that a primary objective was the need to feel important. Children who are abandoned, neglected, or abused receive messages of unimportance. These children, apart from God, may spend the rest of their lives attempting to alleviate those feelings. They may become performance-driven workaholics or insecure, fearful failures. From the Garden of Eden to the present, man has always wanted to feel special and significant. Every person is born with an emotional and mental need for significance, and will spend his life attempting to meet it.

So, the need for love, security, and significance are man's major goals. One tends to revere and honor whatever satisfies his needs, deeming it precious in his heart and life. If God is not the source of these needs, this highly favored assignment goes to another. This circumstance positions God in competition. The result is idolatry, which jeopardizes all areas of one's life. A person is out of order when he satisfies his needs selfishly and apart from God. This very serious aberration of God's plan produces an assortment of relationship abuses that perpetuate themselves within a family from one generation to the next.

With these thoughts in mind we will, in the next chapter, explore some of the common relationship abuses and difficulties, which arise from seeking to meet our basic needs in the wrong way.

The Fruit of Relationship Abuse:

Part II–Overcoming Unhealthy Personality Traits

Chapter 13 Ann Billington

Man has a God-designed need for love, security, and signifi-cance. Relationship with God and man is the intended means through which God expects us to satisfy those needs. However, a variety of relationship problems arise whenever man attempts to satisfy his own needs for love, security, and significance through himself or other relationships apart from God.

As we begin to understand how to walk in a healthy depen-dence, first upon God and then people, to get our inner needs met, we must understand some of the dynamics of relationship abuse. There are five basic personality types who experience common relationship problems. Understanding these five personalities will not only help us to recognize and deal with our own problems, but it will also enable us to recognize destructive tendencies in others as we also learn to avoid the inherent problems.

1. The "Peace at Any Price" Personality

These individuals are compliant people. Frequently, they are people who were raised by aggressive parents who controlled them by using a combination of guilt, rejection, and condemnation to assure proper behavior. For compliants, "no" is the hardest word in the English language. These individuals so fear rejection that they will go to great lengths to please people, sometimes at the expense of their own convictions. Unfortunately, they are an easy mark for selfish people who might use or abuse them. Most people who are compliant don't realize the fact that their inbred insecurities attract abusers to them. Their inability to say "no" complicates their lives and places them on a treadmill of nonstop performance. This was Jamie's problem.

At first glance, you wouldn't think Jamie was compliant, as she busily orchestrated the final details of the Renewing Romance Dinner for couples at her church. Every move she made revealed efficiency, self-control, and poise. The volunteers under her charge moved quickly and respectfully at her directives. Having worked in the church for years, her character and talents were highly regarded by the leadership.

However, Jamie was a compliant individual. "No" was not in her vocabulary. If you needed a meal prepared and delivered to the sick, call Jamie. If you needed a substitute for the nursery, call Jamie. If you needed a chairman for the Ladies' Spring Banquet, call Jamie. If you needed a dozen cupcakes for a school party, call Jamie. Jamie's home became disordered and chaotic. Jamie was in the grip of performance. Her need for love and significance was so great that she was driven. She felt guilty whenever she said no to people's requests, capitulating easily. Though she was outgoing and presented the appearance of strength and determination, inside she was fearful and timid.

What produced this style of relating in Jamie? She obviously had a personality that appeared to be strong. How did the compliancy develop? Jamie's compliance started early in her life. She was raised by a mother who was controlling and manipulating. Anytime Jamie tried to assert herself, her mother beat her back into compliance with a combination of rejection, condemnation, and guilt. Jamie learned early that to achieve love, security, and significance, she must buckle to her mother's demands and standards of behavior. As an adolescent, she rebelled, left home, dropped out of church, and married. After the birth of her first child, Jamie returned to church.

Because the dominant authority figure in her life used guilt and rejection to control her, Jamie developed compliancy in order to feel loved, secure, and significant. Consequently, she felt threatened if she refused any request. Jamie's story didn't end there. As an adult, those same subconscious standards ruled her life, until one day she burned out.

With resentment and bitterness, she withdrew from fellowship and moved to another church. At last count, she was at her third new church. Rather than dealing with her overly compliant personality, she moved each time she had enough. Jamie feared rejection so much that it caused her to have a gripping fear of confronting another person. Instead, she tried to be all things to all people. When that failed, and it always does, she fled to escape the burden of her compliance and the possible rejection of the people around her.

Like Jamie, a controlling mother who used guilt and rejection to manipulate his behavior raised Scott. However, Scott's mother took control a step further in that she allowed Scott no personal space. Consequently, as a married man, Scott developed difficulties with his wife, June. They constantly battled over Scott's refusal to stand up to his boss. His employer made excessive demands on Scott's time by expecting Scott to work overtime without pay.

Scott was a talented homebuilder, who produced excellent and inventive work. However, not only did his employer exploit Scott, but he frequently took credit for many of Scott's creative innovations. This situation infuriated June. She couldn't understand why Scott wouldn't confront his boss. Not only did he refuse to challenge his boss, but he made excuses for him and defended his boss's selfish behavior. Scott was a loyal devotee of the adage "peace at any price." He avoided conflict at all cost.

As if Scott's pacifying his boss wasn't enough, Scott indulged the same attitudes concerning his mother and father. His mother took the position that no one was good enough for "Junior" and seemed to never miss an opportunity to drive that point home with June. As the innuendoes and underhanded insults flew, Scott passively tuned out. June frequently left his parents' home feeling hurt and violated. When she begged Scott to intervene, he took the peacemaker role, explaining and defending his parents' behavior.

Scott's mother was particularly meddlesome and manipulative. Throughout Scott's early years, she hovered over him emotionally and physically. She was overly involved in his life, wanting to solve his problems in an effort to make him popular and successful. She coached and drilled him socially and was a participant in all of his decisions. However, Scott's mother didn't stop there. Not only did she violate his relational space, but she transgressed his personal space as well. His mother intruded on him in his room, frequently entering without knocking. Scott had little personal privacy. In short, Scott's mother invaded every area of his life.

During adolescence, Scott feebly tried to resist his mother's violations. She responded with rejection and cold indifference. He never learned that he had a right to personal boundaries. Now, as an adult, Scott conducted his relationships in a similar manner, feeling he had no rights or boundaries. He was paralyzed with a fear of rejection. Consequently, Scott believed his needs for love, security, and significance were jeopardized if he rocked the boat.

Characteristic of compliance is inconsistency. A principal gave me, a new teacher, some practical wisdom on classroom discipline. Within our school were teachers who maintained an orderly classroom by using strict discipline, while others were more relaxed. He believed that whether a teacher was strict or lax was not important, but rather that the teacher was consistent. He maintained that inconsistency destroyed classroom discipline.

A first-year teacher who taught at a high school in a large metropolitan area was ill equipped to handle the "blackboard jungle" he encountered. First, he tried to be the students' buddy. That approach didn't last long, since he quickly lost control. Next, he tried to be very strict, threatening the students with punishment that he had no intention of administering. His classroom was a circus, as the students never knew for sure where he stood in classroom discipline.

Consistency breeds security within a child. If he is disciplined today for leaving the lawnmower out, he knows he will be disciplined tomorrow for the same infraction. However, if a child is disciplined today for leaving the lawnmower out, and tomorrow the same behavior is overlooked, he never knows for sure what will provoke his parents. This inconsistency robs him of his sense of security. Children raised in homes with alcoholic parents sometimes encounter inconsistency. For example, a child might forget to do his chores and receive no discipline. Yet later, he might receive a thrashing because he slammed the door or spilled his milk. In an atmosphere of inconsistency, there are no hard and fast rules or clear boundaries, and this produces insecurity.

> *In an atmosphere of inconsistency, there are no hard and fast rules or clear boundaries, and this produces insecurity.*

As an adult, this same child might attempt to please everyone in an effort to gain the elusive security he missed. Because he had no clear-cut, consistent parameters in his childhood, establishing boundaries later in life might be troublesome. Unfortunately, a fear of rejection will become a motivating influence in his life. However, compliancy was never a part of God's plan for man and must not be confused with genuine humility and submission.

Though Jesus was humble, He was not compliant. Some people view Jesus as a wimp who turned the other cheek and washed people's feet. Nothing was further from the truth. Jesus was special. Though He possessed all the love of God within His heart, He stood up to the most influential groups of Jews in Israel, the hypocritical Pharisees and the Sadducees. They tried to trap Him into error, but they never succeeded. They attempted to sway public opinion against Him, but He never wavered. They beat Him, spit on Him, and ultimately conspired with the Romans to kill Him, but He never recanted on His gospel of love and mercy. Most Jewish leaders rejected Jesus as the Son of God. However, Jesus knew who He was and what He stood for.

Jesus' gentle, meek, and humble spirit must not be confused with compliance. He was strong and firm in His convictions and never compromised His mission on earth by embracing an attitude of "peace at any price." Compliant people must realize that they are not jeopardizing the fulfillment of their needs for love, security, and significance when they establish healthy limits. They must conquer the fear of rejection and stand as Jesus did.

2. The "Jezebel" Personality

Jezebels are controlling and manipulative people. Like the Jezebel of the Bible, these individuals force others to meet their needs. Usually they aren't interested in changing any of their own desires or wishes, but rather endeavor to bend others to their will, using almost any tactic that works. They can run the gamut from outright bullies to subtle, sneaky manipulators. They come in all sizes and shapes.

A controller might be the pushy salesman who refuses to take a polite no for an answer or the quietly deceptive mother who covertly directs the lives of her children. Bottom line, controllers are selfish as they control and manipulate others into meeting their own needs of love, security, and significance.

When I first met Joe and Cara, they were new believers struggling with their marital relationship. Joe, though only twenty-five, was already a successful businessman and earned enough to allow his young wife of twenty-three to stay home with their two children. Many issues in their life were solved when they were saved, yet problems with Joe's mother were still troublesome.

Cara, who had a sweet, gentle, laid-back nature, sat in my den trembling from her head to her toes. She had just ended a phone conversation with Joe's mother. Cara timidly expressed a fear that Joe's mother wanted to destroy not just her marriage but Cara herself. I thought she was surely overreacting, since it's not uncommon for young married couples to feel threatened by in-laws.

Next, Joe came to see me expressing some of the same concerns. He knew, through Scripture, that he was to honor his wife over his mother. Joe's mother never remarried after Joe's father died. Instead, she emotionally invested herself in her children. After Joe left home, his younger sister was killed in an automobile accident, leaving Joe as the only surviving child. He felt sorry for his mother, knowing that much of her behavior was motivated out of fear, loneliness, and pain. He didn't want to hurt a lonely, old woman who had nothing left to live for. Yet, she was exerting inordinate pressure on him to comply with her every demand.

Feeling extremely threatened by Cara, Joe's mother criticized and challenged Cara's fitness as a mother. She demanded frequent access to the grandchildren and insisted the young family visit her regularly. During these visits, eruptions of violence and anger were common. Joe's mother flew into rages if her orders were countermanded. She belittled Cara and attempted to alienate her from Joe and the children, suggesting Joe's marriage was a mistake.

Cara resisted the trend she saw developing and began pressuring Joe to intervene to stop his mother's tyrannical behavior. Joe felt uncomfortably trapped in the middle. He wanted to please his wife, and he certainly wasn't blind to his mother's tactics. However, neither did he want to hurt his mother or be subjected to her wrath. Joe had left home at eighteen to be free of her outlandish conduct, and now he did not know how to arbitrate between his wife and mother.

I found it interesting that Joe didn't realize how abnormal his mother's behavior was. He had lived with it all of his young life, and he assumed everyone's home was like his. Upon realizing that he was not dishonoring his mother by standing up to her and resisting her control and manipulation, Joe, for the first time, refused to buckle under his mother's demands. That act ignited a tirade from his mother in which she accused him of being a rebel and a troublemaker, a favored rationale retrieved from his youth. She blamed him for all of her problems from the time he was small until he "abandoned" her at eighteen. Joe's mother was a classic controller who selfishly manipulated those in her life to meet her own needs.

In observing the habits of controllers, these characteristics are the basis of much of their behavior:

Selfishness

Controlling people are selfish and self-absorbed. They have little interest in meeting others' basic needs, but rather choose to manipulate people into satisfying their needs and wants. They use tactics such as anger, accusation, or subtle manipulation to force compliance. Unconditional love appears to be a foreign concept to them. Rather, love is a weapon to be given or withheld depending on one's performance. Joe's mother wanted life on her terms. Her major ambition was to order the lives of her family to meet her needs for love, security, and significance.

Irresponsibility

Most controllers refuse to accept responsibility for their wrongdoings, preferring to blame others. If they control others in order to achieve their goals, they don't have to deal with their own problems. This is a common concern in marriage. Each party wants the other to change to meet his or her basic needs, absolving the individual from seeing his or her own faults and effecting change. Joe's mother wanted him to take responsibility for all of the problems in the family. If she could manipulate him into accepting this, then she didn't have to evaluate her own behavior and accept responsibility for her sins.

Boundary Violation

Most controllers are fence jumpers. They won't honor other people's boundaries and limits. They push through boundaries to achieve their selfish goals. The compliant person is frequently a victim of a controller's boundary violations. Scott was a classic example of an individual who was never permitted boundaries. His boundaries had been violated so often that he didn't believe he had a right to them. Scott's task was to learn how to establish healthy boundaries.

Unlike Scott, Joe was not a compliant person. He did leave home, in part because he wearied of his mother's intrusion into his life. The only way Joe could achieve any independence was by separation. Then, he could establish personal space and personal sovereignty, a privilege his mother prohibited. Joe, too, was dealing with a fence jumper and had to establish suitable boundaries for the protection of his home.

Rebellion

Controllers sometimes have serious problems with rebellion. Perhaps as children, they didn't want to knuckle under to the restrictions placed on them, so they were forever vigilant for ways in which to circumvent those limits. Perhaps they resisted restraints and authority. Most controlling individuals I have encountered struggle with all forms of authority. Some controllers will flagrantly violate the rules. Other controllers are so bound by performance that they may lack the courage to blatantly break the law, but they might find ways in which to bend it. They are forever searching for loopholes to wiggle through, thus circumventing the rules. Then to complicate the situation, controllers frequently have difficulty accepting responsibility for their actions. Consequently, they can't repent of sin they refuse to admit. Failure to acknowledge and repent of sin is, in and of itself, rebellion.

> *When we are wrong, the Holy Spirit convicts us. He does not condemn us, nor does He use pity to acquire our love.*

Guilt And Self-Pity

Controllers will use alternating messages of guilt and self-pity to manipulate their victims into compliance. Joe's mother used guilt in an attempt to control their confrontations. She wanted him to give in to her because he felt guilty. When that tactic failed, she reminded him that she was all alone in this world, with only Joe to love her. This approach was a combination of guilt and pity, again to illicit compliance. God uses neither guilt nor pity to order our behavior. When we are wrong, the Holy Spirit convicts us. He does not condemn us, nor does He use pity to acquire our love.

Deception

Many controllers are masters of deception. They are victims of deception as well as being deceivers themselves. Since they can't admit wrongdoing, they frequently indulge in denial as they attempt to manipulate those around them. Though it may seem impossible, many controllers do not recognize their behavior as controlling. They are blind to their sin. They can't see that they are playing God in someone's life. Other controllers know exactly the tactics they are employing. However, they believe that the end justifies the means. In other words, they know that they are manipulating, but feel it is for a good reason and a just cause. Therefore, they don't acknowledge their behavior as sin. Since rebellion tends to produce deception, the controller is easily deceived.

Obsessive Performance

Controllers are usually obsessed with performance. The goal of all of their manipulation and control is to gain a particular performance from those around them. They want people to behave in a certain way, so they use control to achieve it. Joe's mother had a standard of performance that she wanted Joe to meet. Basically, she wanted him to perform as a son, husband, and father according to her standards. When Joe resisted, she resorted to whatever behavior was necessary to achieve his compliance.

Controllers can be healed. Usually, some demonic influences are motivating part of their behavior. Most controllers were themselves controlled. They have learned their behavior from their parents. However, fear and pride in the form of self-devotion and selfishness are the roots of their problems. These sins alone reduce, if not eliminate, an individual's ability to have intimate relationships.

Fear is another motivator for control. Many people who have been sexually abused or exploited in some way have learned the art of control and manipulation to protect themselves from what they consider further abuse, while some others have adopted this behavior as a result of an inner vow never to trust or allow anyone close to them. The result of all of these might be problems with control.

Though the demonic, iniquities, and inner vows may play a large role in a controller's problems, sin and self-devotion still remain their worst issues. The only way to freedom is through repentance from pride, self-devotion, and fear. Controllers believe their needs will never be met unless they make it happen. They don't believe that God is big enough to care for them. Being performance-bound people, they may also believe that their performance is not good enough to warrant God's intervention or His love. They don't trust God to meet their needs for love, security, and significance and, therefore, must provide for themselves.

Controllers can certainly claim Jezebel as one of their examples. She was a model of deception as she promoted her own agenda for profit and gain. Selfishness dominated her life as she manipulatively endeavored to meet her own and Ahab's needs. Like Jezebel, controllers exploit people's needs for love, security, and significance to achieve their own goals.

3. The "Avoider" Personality

These individuals are people who fear and avoid feelings and relationships. They usually believe that their feelings are weak and unimportant, or they fear betrayal. Whichever the case, they are most uncomfortable expressing or sharing their feelings with others. These individuals can seem relational in that they are personable and friendly, unless you press in too close. Then, they keep people at arm's length, preferring shallow relationships without vulnerability. This style of relating can be frustrating for friends and relatives.

Intimacy is built through vulnerability and disclosure. As friends or family attempt to draw close to an avoider, they may experience a deep sense of loss and rejection as the avoider withdraws behind a facade of indifference. On the one hand, the avoider may desire intimacy, but refuses to allow anyone in too close to avoid hurt or fear. His heart may cry out for love, security, and significance, but he rejects relationships, one of the avenues God created to satisfy those needs.

This style of relating many times has its roots in deep wounds. Unfortunately, the avoider suffers frustration in an effort to be close to God. Because he has a closed spirit to all relationships, he avoids depth with God as well. The first step an avoider must take toward healing is the risk of intimacy. If he refuses the risk of self-disclosure with his peers, then he will probably refuse the risk of close relationship with God. As the Apostle John says in 1 John 4:20: *"If someone says, 'I love God,' and hates his brother, he is a liar; for he who does not love his brother whom he has seen, how can he love God whom he has not seen?"* (NKJV).

Though this Scripture is discussing love, a principle is presented that holds true for the avoider. The verse raises the question: How can a man love a God he can't see, if he hates his brother whom he can see? In a similar line of reasoning, if an avoider refuses intimate relationship with the people in his life he sees daily, more than likely he will struggle with a relationship with God whom he can't see. In other words, people can usually only go as deep in relationship with God as they can go with their earthly relationships.

4. The "Cold as Ice" Personality

These individuals, unlike the avoider, appear not to have any emotions. Relationships seem to be unnecessary and feelings impossible. Relationship with this individual is usually surface and at times stilted.

One man who fit this profile perfectly was groomed all of his life to be strong and in control. Unlike the controller, he had no interest in dominating others, because he had no interest in other people. Relatives commonly suggested that this man could watch you bleed to death and not shed a tear. Though that statement was an exaggeration, it did contain an element of truth.

As a child, he was raised on a ranch in West Texas. He was of proud pioneer stock that valued strength and independence. When he was two years old, his father put him on a horse. According to his father, it was time for him to grow up and be a man. At his piercing, frightening screams, his mother charged to the corral. In spite of her tearful, pathetic pleas, his father refused to take him off the horse. Thus, this two-year-old began his march into manhood.

He remembers crying for the last time when he was six years old. From the time he was young, he was schooled to value strength above relationship, power over feelings, and independence over dependence. As he learned to deny his needs for love, security, and significance, he also became desensitized to others' needs. He wanted no one to meet his needs and he met no one else's needs. Love was weakness; security was in his own strength; and significance was in himself. An individual like this has learned to turn inward to gratify himself. He requires no one: not God, not man. Some avoiders use work as a method of avoiding relationship. It is not unusual to find workaholics among this group. Because relationships are unnecessary, they will turn to their work or career to meet all their needs for love, security, and significance.

One might credit this man with no feelings. However, this was not the case. He was a master at emotional control. He considered any display of emotion a weakness and kept his feelings under complete intellectual domination. Only when he became stressed was his emotional control endangered, causing infrequent outbursts of anger. His adult children reported that these outbursts seemingly came from nowhere, producing in them a certain amount of fear and insecurity. They recounted that their father would patiently take harassment after harassment; then one day, seemingly out of the blue, he would have enough and explode. After an outburst, it might be months before he erupted again. From the time he was six years old, this man began to completely lose touch with his feelings. Feelings were to be denied, not examined.

Helping an individual of this type to become aware of his emotions is much like playing twenty questions. However, for him to be completely whole, he must reconnect with his feelings and the situations that caused them. Frequently, hurts and wounds, as well as iniquities and demons, lie at the root of problems like this. He has to learn that he is not his own source for love, security, and significance.

The performer is much like the chameleon reptile that changes its appearance to suit its environment. Likewise, the performer becomes whatever is necessary to be accepted and loved.

5. The "Performer" Personality

This individual is forever on stage, living his life to satisfy a fickle audience whose demands change from person to person and from situation to situation. The tendency towards performance is found in many different relationship problems. The controller and the compliant both are likely to suffer from performance. However, anyone caught in the performance trap is a person who, somewhere in his background, learned to perform to achieve love, security, and significance.

Consequently, performers have an identity problem. They many times do not know who they are, what they like or dislike, or how they feel. So, their goals and standards may change from person to person depending on whom they are trying to please or impress. The performer is much like the chameleon reptile that changes its appearance to suit its environment. Likewise, the performer becomes whatever is necessary to be accepted and loved. If he is with a group of people whose morals and standard are different, he might conform rather than be rejected.

A coach we will call Don was just such a person. He had been an athlete all of his life, so the stage for his obsession with performance was set early. His parents lived for his successes, never missing an athletic event. He was a good student and a class leader in high school. His parents reveled in his popularity and success. From his earliest memory, his parents' lives revolved around his performance. They controlled Don by giving and withholding love. When he was "good," they were profuse in their praise and love. However, when he failed to meet their expectations, they withdrew behind a silent wall of disappointment.

This method of control produced insecurity in Don. He learned early to perform properly or be alienated from his parents' affections. This method of control bred obsessive performance. So, not only did Don behave in a way that pleased his parents, he also began to tailor his likes and dislikes to suit them. Don learned how to satisfy not only his parents but also his classmates and teachers alike. He painstakingly learned how to please everyone, thus earning their love and appreciation. Now, as an adult, he has lost himself. He really doesn't know who he is. His identity is what he perceives others want him to be.

Another problem performance-bound individuals have is a fear of failure. Because they believe that love is based on their performance, they live in a perpetual and tormenting fear of failure. When performance-bound people fail at a task, more is at risk than just a failure or mistake. They feel their very life is on the line. To fail means not only are their needs threatened, but also their self-esteem is in jeopardy. With their self-esteem tied to performance, fear of failure becomes a dreaded monster.

Don was a driven man. By the time he was an adult, the seeds of performance were in full bloom. Success became his god, and he sacrificed everything at its altar. As a coach whose win-loss record determined whether he kept his job, he worked night and day, seven days a week. Losing a game was unacceptable, because it was more than just a game. His self-esteem and identity were at stake.

The seeds of performance eventually bloomed into the weeds of workaholism. Don was on the threshold of disaster. His wife wanted a divorce; his team was losing; and he was suicidal as he looked down the barrel of failure and defeat. Don, like so many performance-bound people, couldn't separate his performance from his self-esteem and identity. All of his needs for love, security, and significance were tied to his performance.

Unfortunately, performance-bound people transfer their obsession to God. Instead of accepting a relationship with Jesus as a free gift of the cross, they become like the Judiazers in Galatia, who abandoned grace and adopted works. Performance-oriented people believe they must earn God's love and acceptance. Many times they become legalistic as they jump through spiritual hoops in an effort to please God.

Every Christian needs to feel loved by God, secure in God,

and significant to God. However, as long as performance-bound people continue to order both their physical, emotional, and spiritual lives by their achievements, peace will elude them. Like the gerbil on a treadmill, they will charge forward but never escape their cage. Like most of the relationship abuses, attention must be given to the demonic realm, iniquities, inner vows, or hurts. Eventually, however, the performers have to repent of dead works, take their hands off of their own lives and the lives of others, and allow God to be God. Performance-bound people must understand that their behavior usurps God's role in their lives and in the lives of others.

As we understand the dynamics of each of these five common unhealthy personalities, it is also important to understand that most people have a combination of these traits. For example, a compliant person might use obsessive performance and control to manage his life. An avoider might, in the place of intimacy, over-perform and control to meet his needs. So, these abuses can overlap, but the common thread among them is that they are all misdirected efforts to meet the God-created needs of love, security, and significance apart from God.

In the next chapter, we will discuss the key factor in restoring a stable foundation for right relationship. As we understand the reason for wrong relationships and some of the unhealthy traits that can develop in a negative environment, we can finally resolve these issues by understanding the key foundation to restoring successful and fulfilling relationships.

The Fruit of Relationship Abuse:

Part III–Restoring the Foundation of Relationship

Chapter 14 Ann Billington

The previous two chapters discussed several points that warrant review. First, we learned that God created man with the needs for love, security, and significance, and that it was His intention to meet those needs in two ways: through a relationship with Himself and through relationships with others. Next, we learned that man's fall into sin disrupted God's plan, and man began to seek love, security, and significance through his own temporal efforts.

As a result of sin, which produced a selfish preoccupation with his own needs, man fell into a number of relationship abuses. How does a believer go about correcting the abuses he recognizes in his life? Assuming that all the iniquities have been broken, demons delivered, and hurts healed, how does he change a lifetime of behavior and feelings? How does a compliant individual overcome his fear of rejection and become bold and confrontational? How does a controlling person stop destructive behaviors and adopt new relational habits? Now that an individual is free, delivered, and healed, how does he change?

The answer to these questions lies in a personal and intimate relationship with God through Jesus Christ. The first time this answer was given to me, I sat in silence, sarcastically thinking, "That's nice. How does one become intimate with a being that doesn't talk?" However, little did I realize that God *does* talk. The problem was, I couldn't hear.

We understand in our earthly relationships that to be intimate with anyone involves, at the very least, two things—time and communication. Both of these requirements take effort, and that effort requires self-discipline. The same principles hold true in relationship with God. Intimacy entails a time investment that for many seems fruitless and boring. Yet, that is precisely how a relationship begins. At first, it may be slow, but over time it deepens and develops into a meaningful friendship. To enrich our relationship with God, we must spend the time it takes to know Him and recognize His voice.

At first, I found spending time with God difficult. Many of my friends related marvelous times with the Lord, where it seemed they were transported into the third heaven. My prayer times, on the other hand, were boring, laborious, and dead. When I picked up the Bible to read, my mind wandered in every direction but toward God. I thought about the busy day ahead of me and became restless and edgy, wanting to get on with something more productive. So, I disgustedly shut my Bible and went about my day. Once again, I had failed in reaching God. Feelings of condemnation dogged me until I avoided quiet times altogether. They became operations of futility and failure, leaving me discouraged and rejected.

Over time, I slipped further and further from God. I went about the motions of worship, quiet times, and church attendance, but they were hollow and empty. Knowing something had to change, I went before God one morning, crying out my complaint. I opened my Bible to Psalm 25:4-5, which said, *"Show me Your ways, o LORD; teach me Your paths. Lead me in Your truth and teach me, for You are the God of my salvation; on You I wait all the day"* (NKJV).

These two verses epitomized my heart. I wanted to know God's way, and I wanted a relationship with Him in which He would lead and teach me. The word "wait" captured my attention. Looking it up, I discovered it meant, "to await with the notion of holding on strongly; and during the time becoming wound together with the object of the waiting." Simply, it meant that the time I spent waiting for God was not dead, unproductive time.

It didn't matter that my mind wandered and nothing dramatic happened, because I was being wound together with God, even as I waited. This truth helped me to be still and to wait on Him. I learned during these periods that time with God was not a Burger King experience, where you prayerfully placed your order and picked up the answer at the drive-through window. There was no such thing as a speedy, microwave quiet time. I learned to allow God to set the character of our time together. My part in this whole procedure was to be still. Slowly, I began a process of learning to hear God's voice.

At first, the Bible was the only source through which I heard His voice. Verses of Scripture would jump out at me, validating an issue or problem I was considering. I began to journal these experiences so I would have a record of those things I believed God was speaking to me. Even when my mind wandered, I learned to follow it and pray over the areas that just seemed to surface in my consciousness. Later, I would learn that the very issues that wandered into my mind were valid, important, and warranted prayer. Some days seemed more fruitful than others. However, I learned to expect God to communicate with me in some way each day.

Some of the things I heard were disturbing. They involved repentance, which is another step towards intimacy with God. Sin separates us from God, yet the whole purpose of our healing is to deepen our relationship with Him. That task is inhibited by unrepentant sin. To change the way we act, we must first recognize the behavior as sin and repent. The controller must identify his destructive habits, acknowledge it as sin, and repent. True repentance is a humbling experience, and not a casual, perfunctory apology tossed up as an afterthought to God. Rather, repentance involves godly sorrow.

II Corinthians 7:9-10 says, *"Now I rejoice, not that you were made sorry, but that your sorrow led to repentance. For you were made sorry in a godly manner, that you might suffer loss from us in nothing. For godly sorrow produces repentance leading to salvation, not to be regretted; but the sorrow of the world produces death"* (NKJV). Godly sorrow brings great reward in the form of recognition and repentance of sin, and true repentance brings change in a person's life.

Because repentance opens our eyes to our sin and destructive behavior, it also produces humility. When we truly repent without excuses, the facade of pride that has for so long protected our ego collapses. Since God opposes the proud, but gives grace to the humble, the dissipation of our pride removes one more major obstacle to intimacy with God.

In my case, God revealed my sin and I repented. As I grasped

> *Since one form of pride is unhealthy self-love or self-devotion, true love and pride can't coexist.*

the magnitude of the lie I had lived, recognition of enormous pride followed. As I grieved my sin, I also saw that I was not the person I so pridefully believed myself to be. This stage of repentance can be very painful. To see yourself as you really are hurts deeply. For me, it heightened my appreciation of our Savior and my great need for Him.

Since one form of pride is unhealthy self-love or self-devotion, true love and pride can't coexist. The Greek word used in the New Testament for God's type of love is the word *agape.* Agape love is a love based on decision, where sacrifice for others is honored above feelings. God defines himself as love and orders us to love others, a task that is impossible when pride rules our kingdom. When an individual repents and pride is put aside, agape love can take root in his heart.

A controller like Joe's mother was ruled by pride. She attempted to control Joe and his family so her needs for love and security would be satisfied. Agape love didn't steer her life. Pride, in the form of self-love and self-devotion, contaminated her behavior, coloring every decision she made and all the relationships in her life.

Had Joe's mother been ruled by agape love, she would not have violated her son's boundaries. Agape love would have required her to sacrifice her needs in order to do whatever was necessary to produce health and happiness in Joe's life. In other words, the needs of Joe and his family would become more important than her own. Anytime agape love is not the motivating force in a Christian's life, a breach with God will develop. Agape love will not only open doors of intimacy with God, but will produce changes in an individual's behavior.

When a person spends time with God, repents of sin, and rejects pride, intimacy with God deepens. As the intimacy deepens, God's character is revealed through His Word, and His presence is manifest in our lives. As we begin to see His Word work, our understanding and knowledge of God increase, producing confidence in His love for us. 1 John 4:16-19 states,

> *"And we have known and believed the love that God has for us. God is love, and he who abides in love abides in God, and God in him. Love has been perfected among us in this: that we may have boldness in the Day of Judgment; because as He is, so are we in this world. There is no fear in love; but perfect love casts out fear, because fear involves torment. But he who fears has not been made perfect in love. We love Him because He first loved us"* (NKJV).

If we have love for God and man, God abides in us. When love is perfected, fear disappears. We no longer need to fear the loss of love, security, and significance. Perfect love casts out those fears, as God's love fully satisfies our most basic needs. Intimacy with God reveals God's love to us, and we can rest and cease our striving. As a child climbs into the lap of his daddy, we climb into the arms of our Heavenly Father. How fearful can life be when viewed from His lap? How concerned can we be about our needs for love, security, and significance when the One who made us loves us so? Intimacy with God will bring changes in our lives, while meeting our deepest and most important needs.

The end of our journey of healing and deliverance is God. Since the basic problems with mankind began in rebellion to

God and separation from His presence, our fulfillment will only come by repairing that problem. Through faith in Jesus Christ, we are invited to come boldly to God. He loves us deeply and desires a relationship with us even more than we desire one with Him.

Take whatever step is necessary right now to further your relationship with God. Also, make the decision to never give up in your journey to find God. He promises us in His Word that if we seek Him, we will find Him (Matthew 7:7). Not only is that promise true, it is the father-heart of God crying out to us to come home to Him. Only there can we find true and lasting freedom from our past and hope for the future.

The Fruit of Anger & Hostility

Chapter 15 Jimmy Evans

The social landscape of America reveals increasing evidence of anger and hostility. Racism, gang activity, domestic violence, violent crime, and child abuse are steadily growing indicators of anger that we must deal with before they destroy us. Beyond the more volatile and obvious areas of anger in our country, there are some less noticed intricacies of anger that are having just as damaging an effect upon lives.

One of the examples of low-profile anger at work is divorce. Though most divorces don't end up on the front page of the newspaper with some kind of violent finale, they, nevertheless, are the products of deep anger. One marriage counselor I spoke with recently said he believed anger was the number one problem in marriages today. I couldn't argue with him.

Some anger in marriages is the result of problems in the marriage itself. However, much of the anger has nothing to do with one's spouse. The origin of one's anger may be unresolved issues of one's childhood, personal frustrations, or difficulties at work. Whatever the source, when anger isn't dealt with in a proper and timely manner, the result will always be problems—sometimes very serious ones.

This chapter deals with the fruit of anger in our lives and shows how to overcome the negative forces of anger that seek to control us and poison our emotions. To begin with, you will be introduced to three general steps, which we should all learn in order to disarm anger and keep it from controlling us. After that are the "Eight Anchors of Anger" which we must learn to identify and overcome. These are eight specific issues that threaten to tie us to the past issues, people, and events of our lives in an unhealthy way as they fuel feelings of anger and hostility. In learning to pull up these anchors, we will be free from the anger of our past and also free to sail the course of our destiny with emotional freedom.

Three Steps to Victory Over Anger

Probably the simplest and most powerful verses in the Bible concerning anger are found in Ephesians 4:26-27. Here, the Apostle Paul gives straightforward counsel to all who are seeking to live in harmony with God and others. This is what Paul says to those seeking to find victory over anger: *"Be angry, and do not sin: do not let the sun go down on your wrath nor give place to the devil"* (NKJV).

In those two verses, we are given three clear steps to take in order to prevent anger from gaining a foothold in our lives or to remove a stronghold of anger if it exists.

1. Be Angry.

As Christians, one of the most harmful lies we are taught and believe is that we can't be honest about our feelings. Sometimes we think that God will be disappointed or mad at us if we admit our real feelings. Nothing could be further from the truth. Every person is going to feel anger often throughout his lifetime. There is no doubt about that. The only question is, how will it be dealt with?

Jesus felt anger as He drove the traders from the Temple. However, His anger was righteous and was dealt with properly. The Bible gives many accounts of God being angry and of how He deals with His anger. As we learn to get free from anger, we must first allow ourselves to become and feel angry without trying to hide behind a religious mask. That mask doesn't impress God or make the anger go away.

Once we allow ourselves to be angry without shame or guilt, we can then learn to distinguish between healthy and unhealthy anger. Healthy anger causes one to act in a protective manner. For example, if someone tried to kidnap your child, you would become angry and try to stop the kidnapper. If you knew someone was going to try to rob your house or assault you, healthy anger would be the response that would cause you to protect what is yours. The same is true when we feel as if someone we are in relationship with is trying to control or abuse us. Our feelings of anger are healthy feelings that are given by God to prompt a righteous end.

Unhealthy anger promotes destructive behavior. Even when we become angry for good reason, if we don't deal with anger properly, it becomes a dangerous emotion. Going beyond protecting our loved ones, our belongings, or us, unhealthy anger seeks revenge upon its object of wrath. Through the use of verbal assault, emotional harm, financial loss, physical pain or a combination of those, unhealthy anger drives its possessor to inject its venom as deeply and as frequently as possible.

This destructive behavior is the reason unhealthy anger is so damaging to relationships. Even when we aren't mad at the people we are with, if we are angry and bitter toward someone else, it will still flavor the relationships of those we are around and cause us to manifest the fruits of our anger that inevitably spill out on those we care about the most. Not only does such unhealthy, destructive anger harm those around us, but it also harms us. I heard someone say it like this: The poison of destructive anger damages the vessel it is stored in worse than anything it can be spilled upon.

Regardless of the cause of our anger, the first thing we must do is admit that we are angry. Without feeling guilty about how we feel, we begin to gain freedom from anger by simply allowing ourselves to feel it. The words, "I feel angry" or "That really makes me angry," would set millions free today if they would only allow themselves to honestly express what they have been feeling for months or years. Some of the most destructive and angry people I've ever met are well-intentioned people who bottled up their anger until it finally exploded. No matter how much anger is in you, begin now to be honest about all of the anger you feel and about each new element of anger as you become aware of it.

2. Do Not Sin.

Paul cautions us concerning the way we allow those feelings of anger to direct us once we are willing to be honest about our anger. The most critical step in keeping anger from becoming destructive is by submitting it to the Lordship of Jesus Christ. As we admit our anger, whether it is healthy or unhealthy, the next step to freedom is to give our anger to Christ.

According to Hebrews 4:16, we are encouraged to come boldly before God's "throne of grace" with every issue and problem in our lives. We are promised by the writer of Hebrews that we will receive sympathy from Christ, who was tempted in all manner like us, yet without sin. We are also promised that as we take our problems to Jesus, we will receive the grace we need for each situation. In other words, Jesus is ready and willing to give us exactly what we need to deal successfully with every problem in our lives, if we will have faith in Him and His desire to give us grace.

Each one of us is too weak within himself to handle the problems of his life. Much of the destruction in our lives can be traced to an unwillingness to trust God with our problems and pains. If we would just trust Jesus to love us, forgive us, and guide us in every trial, He would. The result would be that we would live lives of success and blessing. Related to anger, we must learn to take our feelings of anger and bring them openly before God's throne in prayer.

As we are honest about our anger and we deal with it in prayer, Jesus is faithful to dispense His grace. Sometimes this means He directs us to His Word to give us information that will enlighten us about His will. In other cases, God's grace for anger means He heals our wounded emotions and replaces the anger with His love. At other times, God directs our anger toward loving but truthful confrontation to resolve and redeem a situation. Still at other times, God will take our anger and turn it into spiritual warfare to pray God's will for a person and/or situation that needs passionate intercession.

> *Much of the destruction in our lives can be traced to an unwillingness to trust God with our problems and pains.*

We need to remember that God's grace will manifest in some way, as long as we take our anger honestly before Him and submit it to Him. True submission reveals itself by our willingness do anything God tells us to do with our feelings, even if what He says goes totally against them. An example is in the sixth chapter of Luke where Jesus commands us to love our enemies and to pray for those who mistreat us (Luke 6:27-28). If our prayers to God are simply asking God's divine endorsement on our carnality and plans for "righteous revenge," God will have no part in this false submission. However, if we are truly submitting to God, we will do what He says to do. If we obey, true and lasting freedom will be the result.

3. Do Not Let the Sun Go Down on Your Wrath, Nor Give Place to the Devil.

The first two steps of dealing with anger focus on the "hows" of doing it. The final step deals with the "when." Simply put, we must decide by an act of our will, never to go to bed angry. Taking this advice would save many marriages. Some of the healthiest married couples I know are people who have committed never to go to bed angry at one another. Even if it means talking for hours, they are committed to resolving every issue before going to sleep. This isn't just smart; it's biblical.

Whenever we allow ourselves to go to bed angry, there are two dangerous things that begin to happen. First, our anger begins to sink more deeply into our subconscious mind. In fact, it's not unusual to wake up in the morning and forget much of the reason why we were angry in the first place. What is important here isn't the fact that we can't remember details, but rather, how our unresolved anger affects our overall disposition and attitudes toward the person at whom we are mad.

Many people have the basic philosophy regarding anger that they should "sleep on it" for a day or two and then handle it. Though there may be great wisdom in not dealing with a person until one is in control of one's emotions, it is unwise to indefinitely ignore anger. Even if there is not an immediate confrontation, one must still get anger out and deal with it before God. If this doesn't happen, anger will have a negative impact upon one's life. People who often sleep on their anger, carry with them, as a part of their overall disposition, a noticeable level of hostility. This level of hostility will fluctuate depending on their ages and the severity of the problems in their lives. However, it is always present and manifests itself in every area of their lives.

Second, unresolved anger gives the devil access to our emotions. Paul is careful to tie together the issue of letting the sun go down on our anger with giving the devil a foothold. I'm not sure the exact level of access the devil and his demons have into our thought lives. However, I'm sure they do have entry into it. The devil knows when one is wrestling with feelings of resentment, bitterness, and even hate. Not only that, he has six thousand years of experience in dividing relationships and destroying lives. According to the Bible, he is a liar, an accuser, and a murderer (John 8:44 and Revelation 12:10).

When we allow anger to settle into our minds and hearts, demonic voices soon begin to fan the flames of resentment into red-hot emotions of hatred and revenge. Replaying every negative event that led to our anger, the devil licks our self-pitying wounds as he supplies us with "information" to help us build an airtight case against our enemies. Once we have bought into his way of dealing with anger, he then has a foothold into our lives. He will use that foothold to control our thoughts, speech, and actions until we are liars, murderers, and accusers, just like him.

I've found, over the years, that people who are genuinely sweet, loving, and loyal all have the same thing in common— they refuse to allow anger to lodge in their minds and hearts. Their sweetness isn't due to heredity or stupidity; it is because they treat anger as a toxic chemical. Even if it began as a righteous emotion, they treat the product as something too dangerous to be stored within them. Through daily, decisive action, they have learned to keep themselves free from destructive anger. The result produces people with whom others want to be and with whom one can build a good relationship. The devil has no foothold within them that he can use to harm them or those around them.

The Eight Anchors of Anger

Now that we have learned the three basic steps in dealing with anger, I want to elaborate on some of the most common issues we must deal with while overcoming anger and hostility. These eight anchors are the main reasons most of us experience anger. In being set free from anger, we need to learn how to recognize the reason for our anger and the way for specifically pulling up that anchor. These eight anchors are specific issues we need to learn about in order to successfully implement the three steps we learned from Ephesians.

1. The Anchor of Unforgiveness and Unbroken Judgments

When I first began my ministry in marriage counseling, a young couple came for premarriage counseling. The bride-to-be quickly mentioned her fiancé's frequent outbursts of anger. Even though he rationalized and minimized everything she said, I refused to continue counseling until he became honest about his anger and was willing to deal with it.

We began to search for the root causes of his anger. Our search ended when he admitted his deep hatred for his father. It hurt him so deeply that he found it very difficult to speak about. Soon, after admitting how deeply his father had hurt him, he cried harder than almost any man I have ever seen. I felt very sorry for him. However, his tears were healing. As he forgave his father and broke the judgments he had placed on him, he pulled up an anchor that had tied him to the hurt of his past. In the weeks that followed, this young man and his sweet fiancée found that the anger within him disappeared. They couldn't believe how different he was when he decided to forgive.

In the second section of this book, there is a complete chapter on the issue of forgiveness and the process of forgiving. If this is something you are struggling with, I would encourage you to refer back to that chapter. The main point is that unforgiveness and unbroken judgments on people in our past cause anger today. The more people we resent and judge, the more angry and hostile we become. Even if the people we haven't forgiven are outside of our immediate family and are far into our past, the fruit of the unforgiveness will still be anger in the present. That anger will affect those we love in a negative way. Forgiveness is essential, not only in receiving the forgiveness of God, but also in receiving freedom from its harsh consequences.

2. The Anchor of Loss and Hurt

One of the stages of grief that people almost always go through when they lose a loved one is anger. The closer the loved one was to us, the more intense our anger can be. We need to understand that this anchor of anger is normal. Anger related to loss or hurt is something normal and healthy people feel. It only becomes negative when one never resolves his loss or hurt.

It is common for people who lose a loved one to become angry with the one who died. Feelings of loss, abandonment, and loneliness fuel this anger. Anger is even more intense and resolution more difficult if the death resulted from smoking, other health abuse, or suicide. Even if one didn't lose a loved one through death, the loss of a relationship through rejection, betrayal, or divorce still causes feelings of anger.

In addition to feeling angry with people when we lose them, it is also common to become angry with God. "Why did You allow this to happen?" is the main question that streams from the wounded heart to God. Though the person who is angry with God may realize how wrong his anger is, it is still present. We don't need to feel bad about the emotion; we simply need to learn to be honest about it and bring it to God.

The answer to being free from the anchor of anger caused by loss or hurt is to resolve it. If we have lost loved ones through death, we must reconcile the issue by surrendering them into the hands of God. Thanking God for the time He gave them to us, we trust God with their eternity and ours. Without surrendering our loss into God's hands and resolving our emotions through trust, we will forever be tortured by anger and a variety of confused and unpredictable emotions.

This principle is true regardless of the manner in which we manifest hurt. Whether our anger is directed toward parents, marital partners, friends, or God, we must come to the point where we can trust God to resolve the situation in them and us. This step is critical in finding freedom. Faith in God's love and sovereign power is the key to finding the resolve we need to be able to let go and go on.

3. The Anchor of Fear

Sometimes anger is caused by what we fear. If we fear failure, rejection, sickness, death, or something else, we will almost always become angry at the objects we believe are bringing about the things we fear. I experienced this fear when I went into the ministry. Without admitting it, I was very fearful of failing. After spending ten to twelve hours a day trying to succeed at work, I would come home to an angry wife.

Rather than being sympathetic with my zealous pursuit of success, Karen was annoyed that my heart wasn't turned

> *An interesting result of trusting God is that people won't have as much influence over our lives as before.*

toward her or our children the way it should have been. The more Karen resisted my attempts to be successful by overworking, the angrier I became at her. Without realizing it then, I feared that Karen's resistance would keep me from working as much as I should, which would result in failure. Because I feared it so much, I became angry with Karen or anyone else who resisted my success.

Once again, the answer for fear is trust in God. I had to come to a point where I trusted God for my success and stopped becoming angry with people. Once I did that, I was able to turn my heart toward home the way I should have, trusting God with my success. We must also trust God with our health, our future, our finances, and every other issue in our lives. There are times when we might need to stand up to a person for our own good. However, if we are trusting in the Lord, we will be able to do so without harming them or ourselves. An interesting result of trusting God is that people won't have as much influence over our lives as before.

4. The Anchor of Ignorance

I know one man who can climb mountains and skydive without a trace of fear. However, he is terrified of women. The reason for his fear is ignorance. Because as he grew up, he was not instructed in how to understand women, his ignorance fueled several bad experiences. As a result, this man refuses to relate to women beyond the most superficial level, and he feels a great deal of anger related to women in general.

I feel the same way about swimming in the ocean. I've visited the ocean only a dozen times in my life. I am ignorant about what to do or what to expect, which produces fear in me. Though I feel that way, Jacques Cousteau could be swimming next to me in the ocean having a great time. The difference between us is knowledge. After a lifetime of training, he knows every species of "critter" around him and what they can and cannot do to him. He is familiar with the nature of the ocean currents and how to deal with them. The result is calm and confidence. However, the same sharks he "respects," I "hate" and "fear."

In an atmosphere of ignorance, we can become angry, prejudiced, unreasonable people. The young man who could skydive without concern, but responded to women with fear and anger, needs to learn the nature of women. By increasing his knowledge and understanding of the female gender, his ignorance and anger could be turned to respect and love. Though studying sharks "up close and personal" is not my life's goal, the same principle holds true.

When we have a chronic anger in our lives, one of the questions we need to ask ourselves is whether our anger is fueled by ignorance. Do we really understand what is causing our frustrations? If we made a concerted effort to become knowledgeable, would it change our demeanor? If we will admit our ignorance and seek knowledge as we honestly answer these questions, the result will be less anger and more peace, internally and externally.

5. The Anchor of Spiritual Harassment

Early in our marriage, Karen and I went through a three-day period fighting about everything. At the end of the third day,

Karen asked me if we were going to our weekly Bible study. I told her she could go if she wanted, but I wasn't going. Without further discussion, she went.

When Karen came home that night she urgently related this story. At Bible study, the woman who headed up the group with her husband asked Karen where I was. Of course, being as honest as she is, Karen admitted to her that we were fighting. This lady, in response to Karen's information, related a vision God had given her earlier that day concerning our home. In her mind, she saw a lion roaring into our living room; he was seeking to cause confusion between Karen and me.

Karen repeated this story to me, along with her interpretation of the vision. She believed that the three days of fighting were the result of spiritual harassment from demonic forces. We prayed immediately. This was the first time we had ever confronted the realm of darkness. I could feel an instantaneous and lasting difference in the atmosphere of our home. The days that followed were nothing like the days preceding our prayer.

Even though there are times in marriage when our conflicts can be the result of legitimate issues that we need to discuss and resolve, there are also times when our emotions are the result of spiritual manipulation and harassment. In those times, the only answer is to take authority over demonic forces through prayer, as we bind their activity by the authority of the name and blood of Jesus. Without being challenged, it is possible for satanic forces to produce deep feelings of anger and resentment through nothing more than imagination and irritated emotions. We must learn to be sensitive to this and to quickly take authority over them when we believe they are the cause of our anger.

Remember, Satan hates good marriages, loving families, sweet churches, and productive relationships. He loves di-

> *Refusing to think selflessly or realistically, many angry people constantly lift the standard on life and those around them to a level where failure is inevitable.*

vision, gossip, hate, and revenge. By spiritual harassment and manipulation, he does untold damage to relationships. We must learn to expect his interference as we boldly take authority over his demonic agents by the legitimate authority we have in Jesus Christ.

6. The Anchor of Unrealistic and Selfish Thinking

Surely you've seen children when they don't get their way. Many times they become angry at their parents, siblings or friends, not necessarily because they have done anything wrong, but because they don't get their way. Unfortunately, the same is true of many adults. Something I've noticed about chronically angry people is that they are almost always people with unrealistic and selfish expectations. Refusing to think selflessly or realistically, many angry people constantly lift the standard on life and those around them to a level where failure is inevitable. In fact, there is nothing more certain than the fact that life is brutal to those who are selfish and unrealistic.

In order to free ourselves from unnecessary anger, we need to evaluate how selfish and unrealistic our thinking may be in every major area of life. Regarding work, children, marriage, church and other major areas of life, we should be honest with ourselves as to our motives and ideals. In so doing, we would see that some of our anger and frustration is caused by the way we think. Our idealistic standards for others and our selfish perspective of life drive a wedge of frustration between the real world, the world we are so desperately trying to create, and us.

A spirit of servanthood is the opposite of selfishness. A servant is one who serves others regardless of the circumstances. Expecting problems and pitfalls, this person puts a high expectation on himself to serve the Lord and a low expectation on others to reciprocate. Consequently, this person is poised for success. If life becomes disappointing, he is prepared. If life turns out well, he is blessed. Because a servant holds these unselfish attitudes, he simply will not react with anger and hostility. Instead, poise and sound character are his anchors. Isn't that the way it's supposed to be?

7. The Anchor of Stress

Stress is an epidemic in America. Trying to have it all and be it all, we have it more and enjoy it less than any generation in the history of the world. Stress robs us of health, relational bonding, and joy. It also causes deep emotional distress. With feelings ranging from exhilaration to depression, the person under stress can feel a wide spectrum of emotions in a short period of time.

One thing is certain about stress—it causes our nerves to be frayed, and it sets us up for frustration and anger. Our anger can be focused on anything from a stalled car on the freeway to our children for playing too loud. The point is that stress causes our emotions to be much more sensitive and volatile than when we aren't under stress.

For the sake of our own health and relationships, we need to constantly monitor our level of stress and realize that it will rob us of joy in life as it also sets us up for emotional outbursts. In taking an inventory of our lives, we need to remove the unnecessary responsibilities and energy—consumers from our schedules that crowd us and put us under undue pressure. Making a list of our true priorities and protecting those priorities from other things that are further down on the list can accomplish this. The top of our list should always include God and our families. With these priorities protected and schedule overload removed, we should be able to live with the greatest degree of satisfaction and the least amount of frustration.

8. The Anchor of Lack of Spiritual Enablement

"I say then: Walk in the Spirit, and you shall not fulfill the lust of the flesh. For the flesh lusts against the Spirit, and the Spirit against the flesh; and these are contrary to one another, so that you do not do the things that you wish. But if you are led by the Spirit, you are not under the law. Now the works of the flesh are evident, which are: adultery, fornication, uncleanness, lewdness, idolatry, sorcery, hatred, contentions, jealousies, outbursts of wrath, selfish ambitions, dissensions, heresies, envy, murders, drunkenness, revelries, and the like; of which I tell you beforehand, just as I also told you in time past, that those who practice such things will not inherit the kingdom of God. But the fruit of the Spirit is love, joy, peace, long-suffering, kindness, goodness, faithfulness, gentleness, self-control. Against such there is no law" (Galatians 5:16-23, NKJV).

In his letter to the church at Galatia, Paul exhorted them to walk in the power of the Holy Spirit and not by the natural inclination of their flesh. Paul knew from personal experience that none of us has the power to walk in the love and character of Christ without the power of the Holy Spirit flowing through his life. According to Paul, we are able to tell when we are walking in the flesh or in the Spirit by the fruits of our behavior.

When we are exhibiting behavior such as "…hatred, contentions and outbursts of wrath…" we can know that we are walking in our flesh and not according to God's Spirit. However, we can also know that we are walking in the power of the Holy Spirit when we are walking in "…love, joy, peace, patience, kindness, goodness, faithfulness, gentleness and self control…"

When we find ourselves becoming angry, we need to ask ourselves whether we are relying on our own strength or on the power of the Holy Spirit. When we are relying on the Holy Spirit's power and allowing Him to fill our lives, we will see immediate fruit. The opposite is also true. Anger produces a spiritual barrenness that cripples our relationship with man and God.

The Holy Spirit enables us as we admit our need for Him daily in prayer and invite Him into our lives. His ministry continues as we submit to Him each area of pain and conflict that we encounter daily and ask His wisdom and power. The people who live with this type of submission to the Holy Spirit and reliance upon Him walk in the incredible emotional stability and endowment only God can bring. Those who don't must rely on their own emotional ability and disposition to get them through life. The result is emotional instability and weakness.

As you learn to detect and disarm anger in your life, you will also learn to live in the peace that only Jesus Christ can bring. Remember, anger is inevitable for all of us. We will experience it many times throughout our lives. The decision of how it affects us is ours. If we will deal with it properly and promptly, anger will have no ability to bind us to our past or to destroy our hopes of a happy future. This is my hope for you. I pray you will overcome every obstacle of anger as you find God's grace for your future.

The Fruit of Depression

Chapter 16 Jimmy Evans

Depression has reached epidemic proportions in America. Every year we see more suicides, drug addiction, alcohol addiction, and professional treatment for depression. Not only is depression becoming an increasing problem, but also it seems that a real and lasting solution isn't possible for many people. Treatment for much of the depression in America today is nothing more than masking the symptoms or training people in how to manage their condition.

There are real answers for depression—answers that go beyond temporary sedation or shallow platitudes. In this chapter, I will give you the five major causes of depression and the way to deal with each one. I believe these five areas are responsible for the vast majority of depression, and learning to deal with each of them properly will result in genuine and lasting freedom.

The Five Major
Causes and Cures of Depression

Chemical and Biogenic Depression

This cause must be dealt with first because it is an important and controversial topic related to depression therapy today. First of all, let me say that I have a deep respect for the medical profession. Discoveries and breakthroughs in the medical and scientific arenas have saved and helped countless people.

One of the more recent discoveries concerning depression has to do with chemical imbalance and deprivation. The human body and brain depend on a delicate balance of a number of important chemicals to keep them functioning mentally and biologically. When this delicate balance is missing, serious emotional and mental problems can result. I have counseled numerous people who were either being chemically treated for depression or whom I referred to a physician to be checked. Though most cases of depression don't require chemical treatment, some do.

If you are suffering from severe or chronic depression, it would be wise to be checked by a physician or Christian psychiatrist. If you have a chemical imbalance, treatment will almost always help you. In addition to helping you physically and emotionally, treatment for chemical disorders can also help you deal with other issues contributing to your depression. As one therapist put it, "It brings you out of the pit, onto a level playing field where you can deal with life."

My concern about chemical treatment is that nearly all of the people I have seen who required chemical treatment for depression have had significant issues of their past that needed to be dealt with. Issues such as abuse, rejection, divorce, business and personal failure, self-hate, and guilt must be confronted and resolved. In fact, it would not surprise me if the reason chemical disorders in people occurred in the first place was because of months or years of internal emotional distress caused by ignoring problems. Long-term mental and emotional struggling has changed the chemistry of their bodies and their ability to function properly. Stress, grief, and anxiety all have very damaging effects on the body if they last for long periods of time.

In recommending chemical treatment for some people, I try to make it clear that it is rarely the sole answer, though it can be of real assistance in repairing the body and dealing with depression. When chemical treatment is combined with counseling to address the deeper issues of one's past and present, it is most successful. In fact, when the deeper issues of one's life are addressed and resolved, the need for continued or long-term chemical treatment may be minimized or removed.

For every person who is dealing with depression, my desire is for your complete healing. I encourage you to seek medical treatment if you think you are suffering from chemical or biogenic depression, as long as you don't abuse it or use it to mask and avoid deeper personal issues. Unfortunately, many people medicated today for depression will never be set free. Though they may be free from some of the problems they experienced without medication, they are still not cured of their deeper underlying problems. This is unfortunate and unnecessary. My heart goes out to them.

Emotional Exhaustion

Our emotions are just like our physical bodies; they are limited in how much energy they have. Physically, all of us understand that we need sleep and rest. However, most of us expect our emotions to be able to operate at high levels without fail. This is unrealistic.

> *After six days of activity and output, we need to replenish ourselves through rest, meditation, and worship.*

One of the Ten Commandments God handed down to Moses was to honor God by observing a Sabbath day of rest. Most of us view the Sabbath day as something a little outdated. Though we respect God and even attend church, to really shut down for one day a week is, well, un-American! We need to be playing sports, going to the mall, screaming at the TV set as we watch sports—right?

God wants us to enjoy life and live it to the fullest. However, He also knows that He created us to need a day off to rest physically, mentally, and emotionally. God didn't tell us to honor a Sabbath so He could squelch our social life or punish us. He told us to honor it because we need it. After six days of activity and output, we need to replenish ourselves through rest, meditation, and worship.

I have found, through personal experience, that the more I honor God and His principle of a Sabbath rest, the better I function and the more joy and optimism I feel about life. As a pastor, Sunday isn't a day of rest for me; it's the hardest day of my week. Therefore, I take Friday as a Sabbath of rest. When I take Friday to rest, relax, and replenish, it makes a great deal of difference in my physical and emotional health. I also notice that when I don't get a day to rest, I begin to wear down physically and emotionally. Some of the times I've battled depression most were times when I was going seven days a week without much rest. The longer I went, the less joy I had and the more I battled.

Beyond learning to rest weekly, there are other complications related to emotional exhaustion. Anger is an example. One of the classic definitions of depression is "anger turned inward." When we don't ventilate our emotions in a healthy way and resolve them quickly, they turn inside and begin to consume emotional energy. Anger is a major consumer of emotional energy. We need to understand how damaging anger is to our emotions when we allow it to remain within us.

When we don't forgive, confront, or do whatever is necessary to resolve our anger, it will eventually cause our emotional disposition to change and ultimately collapse. Anger turned inward, first of all, changes our ability to have peace of mind and a general sense of joy. After that, it begins to poison our disposition, affecting those with whom we are at peace. Finally, depending on its level of intensity, anger will sooner or later cause us to become emotionally worn out and exhausted—and so comes depression.

We must learn to be sensitive to anything that is consuming us emotionally and learn to deal with it promptly. In most cases, depression itself isn't the root problem; it is simply a manifestation of something else with which we need to deal. Unresolved anger, stress, anxiety, and grief are all major emotional consumers. When we ignore them or refuse to deal with them, they will eventually deplete our emotional reserves, and depression will be the result.

Beyond the emotional consumers just mentioned, there are the inevitable good times we will enjoy in life that also consume our emotions. One example is childbirth. Though childbirth is a momentous event, we also know that depression is common for the mother after she gives birth, due in part to the chemical changes in her body. However, it is also a result of the tremendous emotional investment required during the birthing process. Postpartum depression is, to some degree, a woman's emotions trying to recover after a great depletion.

Like childbirth, almost every major event in our lives that requires significant celebration, attention, and personal interaction is followed by an emotional letdown. People who win gold medals in the Olympics many times experience mild depression up to several days following the event. The same is true for beauty contestants, athletes, preachers, and people from every walk of life. When your adrenaline is pumping and you are investing yourself emotionally in something good or bad, there must be a recovery period.

People who have learned to listen to their emotions and be sensitive to the ebb and flow of life, live in much greater emotional stability. Allowing oneself to be consumed emotionally by problems, daily responsibilities, and/or special events without understanding the inevitable drain and need for recovery, can result in a constant battle with depression without understanding why.

Some final words of advice concerning depression: Don't let issues eat at you internally. Get them out. Resolve them. Take them to God. Get help from someone. You can't afford to allow them to exhaust you emotionally. Your life and the lives of those around you are at stake.

Plan downtime through the week for your emotions to recover. Don't allow your schedule to be packed too tight. Deal with stress and overload as major enemies of your emotional health, because they are.

Always expect and plan for emotional lows to follow emotional highs. This is a necessary part of emotional health. Just as you wouldn't expect to work your body hard all day with no rest, don't expect it from your emotions either. When your emotions are worked hard, let them rest well.

Unhealthy and Unbiblical Thinking

There are some people who can depress you even if you're not depressed when you see them. These people are always focusing on the negative. They are the proverbial dark cloud looking to attach to a silver lining. These people are depressed and depress others because of the way they think.

All of us need to realize how important our thought processes are. I heard a gifted Bible teacher say once, "A bondage is a house of thoughts." Built around every chronic problem, habit, or addiction in one's life, there is a thought process. Without dealing with the thought life, one won't successfully resolve one's problems.

One of the most significant passages in the Bible concerning the importance of our thought life and how we are to manage it is found in II Corinthians 10. *"For the weapons of our warfare are not carnal but mighty in God for pulling down strongholds, casting down arguments and every high thing that exalts itself against the knowledge of God, <u>bringing every thought into captivity to the obedience of Christ</u>..."* (NKJV) [underline added].

The Apostle Paul was giving the church at Corinth a powerful lesson concerning warfare against sin and Satan. According to Paul, the main arena of warfare with the devil is one's mind. One of the most powerful weapons the devil uses is a person's thoughts. Think for a minute back to the Garden of Eden. What did the devil use to defeat Adam and Eve? Thoughts. Words spoken into their minds caused them to think in an unhealthy and sinful manner. Rather than rejecting those thoughts, they accepted them and acted upon them. The result was the fall of mankind and the introduction of great emotional, mental, physical, and spiritual problems.

In the Scripture in II Corinthians 10, we see that in our battle against Satan we are told to take *"...every thought captive to the obedience of Christ."* This literally means that every thought that comes into our minds must "listen under" Christ. The word of God and the Spirit of Christ within us must be the supreme authorities in our thought lives if we are going to live in freedom. Our worldview, what people say, our natural thought processes, and everything else must submit themselves to what God has to say. If the thoughts agree, they stay. If they don't, they are rejected.

People who battle with chronic depression, suicidal thoughts, and hopelessness almost always have problems in their thinking. The thought processes that lead to serious depression and emotional problems are thoughts that:

- Omit God from the conclusion. The problem is magnified and God is minimized.
- Give no solution or hope. The situation becomes hopeless and final.
- Disagree with Scripture. These thought processes contradict the promises of God and what God's Word says about His love for us and His willingness to forgive and help us.

The fourth chapter of Matthew gives the account of Jesus' battle with Satan in the wilderness. The entire battle was one of thoughts. Satan would throw a lie or half-truth at Jesus, and Jesus would counter him with "...it is written..." This is how Jesus successfully defeated the devil as he sought to destroy Him. We must learn to fight the same way. As Satan and his agents come to deceive us and fill our minds with lies, negative thinking, and unbelief, we must make every thought "listen under" Jesus.

Regardless of how we feel or how logical something sounds, if it doesn't agree with God's Word, we must reject it and accept what God says. Here is what Jesus said to the devil in the wilderness: *"But He answered and said, 'It is written, "Man shall not live by bread alone, but by every word that proceeds from the mouth of God"'"* (Matthew 4:4, NKJV). If our mental diets consist of unhealthy and unbiblical thinking, depression and other serious problems are inevitable. However, if we ingest the Word of God and make it the standard for every area of our thought lives, we will "live" and succeed.

For every problem, there is a solution. That is what God's Word says. God is greater and is bigger than any problem we will ever face. That is what the Bible says. God loves us and is willing to forgive our sins and be our intimate friend. It is written in His Word. There is never a reason for us to give up or lose hope. Negative thinking, hopelessness, and cynicism must be rejected from our lives. The Word of God must be received and believed. As we are careful to scrutinize our thinking and reject those thoughts that are in disagreement with God, we will find victory. Faith is a crucial ingredient to this process. When we decide to believe in God and make Him our answer, clouds of darkness vanish and new avenues of hope will begin to shine before us.

> When we decide to believe in God and make Him our answer, clouds of darkness vanish and new avenues of hope will begin to shine before us.

Spiritual Oppression

"The Spirit of the Lord GOD is upon Me, because the LORD has anointed Me to preach good tidings to the poor; He has

sent Me to heal the brokenhearted, to proclaim liberty to the captives, and the opening of the prison to those who are bound; to proclaim the acceptable year of the LORD, and the day of vengeance of our God; to comfort all who mourn, to console those who mourn in Zion, to give them beauty for ashes, the oil of joy for mourning, <u>the garment of praise for the spirit of heaviness;</u> that they may be called trees of righteousness, the planting of the LORD, that He may be glorified" (Isiah 61:1-3, NKJV) [underline added].

This Scripture passage is a prophetic description of the ministry of Jesus Christ. It describes the redemptive purpose of Jesus' mission into the world. It specifically speaks of how Jesus deals with people who are weighed down with suffering and grief. Verse three states that He gives them, "The garment of praise for a spirit of heaviness."

There are two important truths contained in this verse. The first truth is that depression or "heaviness" is referred to as a "spirit." One of the primary meanings of the Hebrew word *keheh* used for "heaviness" in Isaiah 61:3 is "darkness." This describes depression very well. It is like an emotional darkness that keeps us from seeing hope, answers, or a bright future.

Satan's kingdom is described in the Bible as one of "darkness" (Acts 26:18 and Ephesians 6:12). Satan and his demons are spiritual entities that try to spread darkness across the earth. Beyond his love of darkness, Satan particularly enjoys attacking Christians. He attacks our thoughts, emotions, and environment with as much spiritual darkness and oppression as he possibly can. When we are unaware of his schemes and the way to fight them, the result can be "a spirit of heaviness" that can paralyze us emotionally.

The second important truth we find in verse three is that the answer for a "spirit of heaviness" is the "garment of praise."

Satan hates praise. Praise exalts Jesus. It ushers light and life into our circumstances. It is the ultimate act of faith. The opposite of an atmosphere of praise is an atmosphere of "darkness" and depression. In this atmosphere, no one gets praise, God is hidden and our problems are magnified.

In every situation in our lives, Satan seeks to discredit God and get our eyes off Him. One of the surest signs that he has succeeded is a lack of praise and joy in our lives. Praise is a critical discipline and foundation in our lives that keeps the devil from oppressing and deceiving us. Praise is also a powerful force that repels a spirit of heaviness from our presence (Psalm 149:6) and ushers us into the presence of God (Psalms 22:3 and 100:4).

In learning to overcome depression, we not only need to realize the devil's desire to assault us with a "spirit of heaviness," but we must also realize how important our confession is in defeating him. The words we speak with our mouths are very important. If our words are filled with discouragement and darkness, we have paved the way for forces of darkness to either begin or continue to oppress us. However, if our words are filled with hope, faith, and praise for God, we have opened the door for God to flood our lives with His light and power.

Here are some Scriptures that underline the importance of the confession of our mouths:

Proverbs 18:21: *"Death and life are in the power of the tongue, and those who love it will eat its fruit."*

Matthew 12:36-37: Jesus said, *"But I say to you that for every idle word men may speak, they will give account of it in the day of judgment. For by your words you will be justified, and by your words you will be condemned."*

Hebrews 3:1: *"Therefore, holy brethren, partakers of the heavenly calling, consider the Apostle and High Priest of our confession, Christ Jesus..."* (NKJV).

Through prayer and proclamations of truth and praise, we have complete authority over every spirit of darkness. Don't let the devil or his demons harass you. Regardless of how you feel, how things look, or what anyone says, stand up and begin to praise the Lord and confess the truth of His Word. As you do, darkness must flee and God's light will begin to penetrate your life.

Serious Discouragement

All of us have times of discouragement in our lives. Most of them are normal and are relatively easy to deal with. However, there are other times of discouragement that are more serious. It may be the loss of a relationship, a bad business deal, or something else that sets us back. These more serious times of discouragement can become doorways of demonic oppression and emotional depletion if they aren't dealt with properly.

To help you deal with serious discouragement, I want to direct you to a text of Scripture about David and a time in his life when he overcame incredible circumstances that threatened to discourage him. One of the things I like best about this story is that not only did David reject discouragement, but also "...he encouraged himself in the Lord."

I don't want to teach you how not to be discouraged. I want to teach you how to defeat discouragement and "...encourage yourself in the Lord." The story of David's victory over discouragement is found in 1 Samuel 30. The main elements of the story help us realize the incredible battle David fought to keep from being discouraged.

King Saul was trying to kill David. The Philistines, whom David had been living among, rejected David and told him and his men they could not live among them. As David returned to Ziklag, where he and his men had left their wives, children, and possessions, they found that the Amalekites had raided their camp and taken everything, including their family members. In response to finding their wives and children gone, David's men began to talk about killing David.

Needless to say, David was having a bad day. If anyone ever had reason to be discouraged, it was David. However, David didn't become discouraged. This is something we really need to notice and learn from. You see, discouragement is a decision before it is an emotion. In every circumstance in our lives, we can choose not to be discouraged. Not only can we choose not to be discouraged, but we can reverse discouragement and turn it into encouragement. To learn how to do this, let's continue the story of David at Ziklag and see the three steps he took to "...encourage himself in the Lord..."

> "And David was greatly distressed; for the people spake of stoning him, because the soul of all the people was grieved, every man for his sons and for his daughters: but David encouraged himself in the LORD his God. And David said to Abiathar the priest, Ahimelech's son, I pray thee, bring me hither the ephod. And Abiathar brought thither the ephod to David. And David enquired at the LORD, saying, Shall I pursue after this troop? Shall I overtake them? And he answered him, Pursue: for thou shalt surely overtake them, and without fail recover all. So David went, he and the six hundred men that were with him, and came to the brook Besor, where those that were left behind stayed" (1 Samuel 30:6-9, KJV).

According to the example of David, we defeat discouragement in any situation and encourage ourselves in the Lord by turning immediately to God, seeking the counsel of God, and acting upon God's Word.

Turn immediately to God.

As soon as David finished crying over the news of his family being taken captive, he began to seek the counsel of God. One of the reasons discouragement roots in our minds and hearts is that we turn it inward and meditate on it.

One of the things I have had to learn is to not allow discouragement resulting from bad news or circumstances to turn inward and consume my mind. Before I learned to do this, I constantly battled discouragement. Just as I was over the last battle, something else would take me down. My basic problem was that I tried to figure out how to solve my problems without turning them over to God. If that didn't work (and it never did) I would then take it to God as a last-ditch effort. This is what many of us do, and it is the reason we struggle with discouragement.

Make up your mind, before discouragement comes, that you aren't going to turn it inward; you are going to turn it toward God. This is the first step David took to insure that he wasn't going to be consumed by his circumstances or emotions.

Seek the counsel of God.

One of the worst things we can do when we are discouraged is to act upon our emotions. They will almost always lead us to the wrong conclusions. David, rather than trusting his emotions, consulted God. This point doesn't require much elaboration. Don't trust your emotions or unbiblical advice. Turn to God for your answers. He can give you the wisdom and strength to lead you out of your situation. Though all we can see is dark clouds above us, He sees the light above the clouds and the path we need to take to lead us out of darkness.

Act upon God's Word.

David didn't just ask God's advice; he took it. It's not enough to pray and read the Bible; the time comes when we must act in faith upon what God's Word says and what God is telling us to do. Rarely does this action feel good or pamper our emotions. In fact, sometimes obeying God is a gut-wrenching ordeal. However, it is the only way we will find victory over our emotions. As David stood up and faced his enemies, the only thing he had to go on was a promise from God, but it was enough.

> *If we are waiting for one-hundred-percent proof before we act, we won't act. Obeying God requires faith.*

If we are waiting for one-hundred-percent proof before we act, we won't act. Obeying God requires faith. People who overcome in life are people of faith. They have made the decision that they will not be ruled by circumstances or emotions. Regardless of what they see or how they feel, they follow God's instructions. David was this kind of person. His proactive behavior led him to victory. The interesting thing about the story of David's victory over discouragement is that in the next chapter, he becomes king. Many times, our greatest battles precede our greatest victories and blessings.

I hope this chapter has helped equip you to face and overcome depression. God's desire is for you to have joy and hope in every area of life. He is with you now, and as you turn to Him, He will help you find emotional victory and peace. I pray God's richest blessing upon you as you learn to overcome depression and to live in the joy and encouragement of the Lord.

The Fruit of Addiction

Chapter 17 Ann Billington

Addiction is a heartbreaking condition that not only damages the life of the addict, but also harms those intimate with him or her. No one is addicted without harming others in his life as well. For that reason, both are victims and need ministry. Addiction can be defined as a person's attempt to artificially meet his own needs apart from God. It can take the form of food, relationships, drugs, alcohol, or work, to mention just a few. However, addiction indicates need and habit, where the individual becomes dependent and requires these addictions to survive physically or emotionally, or both.

A dysfunctional family, that is, a family whose members relate to one another in an unhealthy way, usually creates an addict. The dysfunctional family employs destructive behaviors in an attempt to have their basic needs of love, security, and significance met. The further a family strays from the biblical principles in ordering their relationships, the more dysfunctional the relationships will be. These families produce a broad range of problems including compulsive behavior. Because the families lack the warmth, leadership, and love required to produce healthy people, a whole host of destructive behaviors are implemented to avoid pain, which is the primary goal of hurting people. Drugs and alcohol are two methods used by many to deaden that pain.

> *No one intends to become addicted.*

Unfortunately, in the process of deadening their emotional pain, some people develop life-controlling addictions. While many people manage their lives in moderation, being able to use substances without abusing them, others tend to live their lives in excess. They might be presented with the same opportunities or problems as a healthy person, but feel compelled to drink excessively or abuse a substance as a result.

Two of my high school friends decided to experiment with cigarettes. All summer they drove country roads, smoking. In September, one decided smoking was unwise and quit, while the other continued. Eventually, the smoker's habit became a three-packs-a-day addiction that controlled her life for the next twenty years. Her addiction determined which restaurants she patronized, which church she attended, and where and how long she shopped. Addiction became the focus or hub around which her life revolved. The first girl managed her life with moderation and felt no compulsion to continue smoking, while the other became addicted.

No one intends to become addicted. The workaholic doesn't set workaholism as a life's goal; it just seems to happen. The same is true for alcoholics or drug abusers. When they took that first drink or smoked their first marijuana cigarette, they didn't believe drugs or alcohol would become their master.

Every addict I have ever known never intended to become addicted. Yet, each one was in a life-controlling situation, unable to break free. Without knowing, they passed through the stages of addiction, unaware they were on a highway to misery and bondage.

The first stage of addiction is experimentation. This is the level where many young people are captivated by alcohol or drugs. In visiting with teenagers regarding their drug or alcohol usage, a great number say they drank or used drugs the first time because they were curious. Some allowed peer pressure to influence them. Likewise, many addicts took that first drink just to see what it was like. In this stage, drinking or drugs are fun and unique. The users perceive no sense of danger as they move rapidly toward the second level of addiction.

Stage two is characterized by an unconscious acceptance by the users of alcohol, drugs, and other harmful substances as a part of their lives. They are no longer experimenting to discover and learn if drugs or alcohol are for them. Rather, they now embrace the drug as their own, and a lifestyle is developing around that decision. Now these individuals will be at parties freely indulging in drinking or using. However, people in stage two sense no danger in their activities, because they believe they are very much the master of their lives.

People in this stage contend they are in command of the substance and can stop using it at any time. Many addicts report that this time was the happiest for them. They considered their usage recreational and an activity they greatly enjoyed. The drug alleviated numerous problems, such as timidity and insecurity, but had not yet reached the destructive level that addiction brings.

Stage three sees an increase in drug or substance usage and its importance in the lives of the users. No longer can they just take it or leave it. They are developing an increased desire for the substance. In stage two they accepted it as a part of their lives, believing they were in complete control. They set limits and boundaries, and believed they were invulnerable to addiction. In stage three, casual usage becomes obsession. By definition, obsession is a compulsive preoccupation with a fixed idea. At this stage, they are preoccupied with the substance they are abusing, and it is beginning to take control of their lives. The acquisition and use of drugs, alcohol, or other substances occupies much of their thought life, and has become their chief priority.

Stage four is the point of deepest addiction. Users are no longer simply compelled to consume their substance, but it controls them. Their lives are no longer their own. They are in bondage to a cruel master. Because they are physically and emotionally addicted to the substance, their world not only revolves around their use of it, but also the use of the substance has become their life. At this stage nothing and no one is as important as their "drug," and they will sacrifice everything and everyone to use it.

I visited with a lady who was addicted to cocaine. Her habit out-stripped her capacity to supply it by conventional means. She resorted to prostitution. It didn't matter that she was risking AIDS or hepatitis. She was fully aware of the hazards but did not flinch when she inserted a used needle into her arm.

At this stage, only acquisition and use of the addictive substance is important. Who gets harmed in the process is immaterial. Addicts at this stage will do almost anything to supply their habit. They will use and abuse their families and will steal to support the drug because nothing is as important as the addiction. Life does not exist beyond the next "fix."

For addiction to be successfully treated, healing and change must occur in four areas: physical addiction, healing of emotions, lifestyle, and maturity. Physical addiction must be addressed before other issues such as unhealthy relationships, damaged emotions, or toxic thought-life problems can be worked through.

With physical addiction, the body becomes the slave of the drug. This bondage must be broken before healing can go on in the other areas. At the insistence of his parents, a teen addict came to see me. He was so "loaded" that he could not sit straight in the chair. Nothing we talked about got past the drugs. No change could occur in his thought-life, emotion, or behavior until he stopped the drug usage. It is imperative that addicts take steps to break the hold addiction has in their bodies. When a person is chemically addicted, that drug reigns over his existence. However, accomplishing this task is sometimes easier said than done.

I have talked to former drug addicts whom God has sovereignly delivered from addiction. They report being instantaneously set free without another moment's desire for drugs or alcohol. Though I realize this happens, most individuals at stages three and four need a drug treatment program to manage detoxification from the chemical. This isn't to discount the power of God, but simply to say that as we seek His help, He chooses how He will do it. For some, instantaneous healing is His perfect will. For others, God chooses to use human instruments through a process and a period of time to do it. We need to seek God first and then be sensitive and obedient to His direction.

Before going on the next point, let me also stress the importance of support groups during and after recovery. Pastors, psychologists, and drug treatment professionals have all found a common respect for the power of support groups. This isn't a newfound truth because the Bible has been telling us for centuries how we need each other. Over and over, the Word of God addresses our need to love and support each other when we are weak and have need of the strength of fellow believers. What our society is finding out today is the power of this truth. Even though support groups prove to be effective on all levels, the most powerful support mechanism in the world is fellow believers committed to pray for us and support us. To aid addicts in their quest for freedom, as well as providing the encouragement and accountability to stay free, support groups are invaluable.

The second area that must be addressed before total healing is achieved is the repairing of emotions. Few addicts become addicted just because they like the "rush" the substance produces. People will do almost anything to avoid pain. Most dysfunctional families produce emotional wounds. This pain is frequently produced through rejection, which creates a poor self-image and shame. The three basic needs of mankind are love, security, and significance. Every human being was created to require the satisfaction of these three needs.

Dysfunctional homes fail to provide the family members with fulfillment of these needs. This deficit will ultimately be revealed as pain in the heart of the addicts. Therefore, one of the greatest benefits of drugs and alcohol to the abusers is its anesthetizing effect in reducing the pain of hurts and wounds that are produced by a dysfunctional home. Addictive substances alleviate the pain of insecurities, inadequacies, and disappointments, to mention just a few. Under the influence of drugs or alcohol, shy, insecure people become the life of the party. In short, the addicts' lives don't seem so harsh or unmanageable after they have learned to rely heavily on the compensation the substances provide.

Joe was the product of such a family. His father, though not an alcoholic, was abusive and rejecting. Since his father was abusive, all three needs in Joe's life were neglected. As an adolescent he began to drink. By eighteen, he was experimenting with drugs. Today this man is forty years old. He no longer uses drugs, but is a full-blown alcoholic. Rather than deal with his problems, he learned early that the pain of rejection, his poor self-image, and his shame could be anesthetized with drugs and alcohol. When relationships became too complicated or too painful, he disappeared into a bottle, alleviating all his anxiety, anger, and inadequacy. Life then became manageable. For this man to ever experience freedom, he must be healed from the feelings resulting from his father's neglect. The pain must be dealt with for there to be real freedom.

Some alcoholics achieve sobriety but fail to deal with their pain. Consequently, they become "dry alcoholics" who are, by my definition, people who have kicked their addictive habit but still function within their relationships as addicts. They do not use chemicals to control their pain. Instead, they manipulate and control relationships to alleviate feelings of inadequacy. Breaking the physical addiction is only a partial victory. Addicts need to recognize their unhealthy methods of managing pain and allow God to lead them through the process of healing.

> ...one of the greatest benefits of drugs and alcohol to the abusers is its anesthetizing effect in reducing the pain of hurts and wounds that are produced by a dysfunctional home.

The third area that an addict must change is his lifestyle. When a person reaches stages three and four in addiction, a lifestyle will develop, reflecting the character of the addiction.

The lifestyle comes complete with relationships and thought patterns built upon substance abuse.

A heroin addict explained to me the enormous struggle he had in changing his drug lifestyle. He had been clean a number of months without a slip-up. He was using methadone, a drug prescribed to him to block the craving for heroin. In his opinion, the physical addiction was not his big battle. Because of methadone, he had no physical craving for the drug. He maintained that restructuring his lifestyle was his big battle. While he was on drugs, his life revolved around the acquisition and usage of drugs. Every morning for years, he had awakened with only one concern on his mind—how to get his daily "fix" of heroin. The entire day was devoted to that goal. Now that it was no longer necessary to acquire heroin, he expressed an emptiness and lack of purpose that he found difficult to alleviate.

Where the average person awakens, goes to his job, relates to his family, and sets goals for his life, a heroin addict's life's ambition is to supply that day's dosage. In many cases it matters little to him how he accomplishes that objective. To change his lifestyle, new goals and direction must be established.

As a part of a lifestyle change, the addict must also develop new and healthy relationships. It is impossible for him to stay "clean" while constantly being in the company of users. Every addict must distance himself from those who persist in drug or alcohol usage. Because of man's need for new relationships, life for the recovering addict may feel lonely. He will need a new community, new friends, and in some cases a new family.

Unfortunately, the addict most often comes with a host of co-dependents, who are friends and family members who have enabled him to use or drink freely without responsibility or repercussion. Co-dependents can take the form of a well-intentioned mother who rescues her son from the consequences of his actions or a spouse who suffers abuse over and over while providing financial and emotional support to the addict. Not only does the recovering user need to change, the roles of the co-dependent must also change. This task is challenging, but it is essential for the healing of the addict and those around him.

As a part of the change of lifestyle, the addict must also change the way he thinks. To change one's life requires a new thought-life as well. The only way to effectively change thought-life is to experience a heart change. Proverbs 23:7 says, *"For as he thinks in his heart, so is he"* (NKJV). Christianity is the only religion in the world that changes a man's heart and renews his mind. Jesus took a hardened persecutor of his followers named Saul; touched his heart, and made him the greatest apostle to the Gentile world. In other words, addicts have been consumed with one goal and pursuit—acquisition and usage of drugs or alcohol. All thought-life has revolved around those ambitions. When those pursuits cease, the addict's thought-life must change as well. No longer can he think about drugs and old endeavors. If he does, his thought-life will draw him back into addiction. For an addict to reminisce about the old days is an invitation to failure, and a luxury he can't afford. He must develop not only new goals and healthy relationships, but new thoughts as well.

II Corinthians 10:5 says man must be *"'casting down arguments and every high thing that exalts itself against the knowledge of God, bringing every thought into captivity to the obedience of Christ"* (NKJV). Breaking the cycle of addiction requires taking every thought captive to the obedience of Christ. The addict must line up his thinking with the Word. I do not believe he can have lasting success unless his heart belongs to Jesus and his thought-life changes. When a person experiences a heart change, he will then begin to think differently. As he thinks differently, his behavior will change.

Satan and his demons also raise their ugly heads in the lives of recovering addicts. Since Satan can affect an individual's thought-life, attention to this area of ministry is important. Addicts in the course of their lifetimes can open several doors to demonic activity. Addicts open the first door by altering their state of consciousness. Once the conscious mind is impaired, it is vulnerable to demonic activity. Dysfunctional homes provide a second open door for Satan. These homes usually produce hurts and traumas. Again, these hurts can open doors for demons to enter. To add to this problem, the addict has also indulged in repeated sin, which opens yet another door for demonic oppression. In short, the lives of chemically addicted individuals are fertile ground for the infestation of demons. Deliverance will be a necessary ministry for the addict desiring to change his thought-life.

Several years ago, a man came to my office fresh out of the penitentiary. He had been incarcerated for three years for possession and dealing of drugs. This was his second trip to prison. While inside, he came to know Jesus as his personal Savior. Though he managed to stay clean while incarcerated, he struggled after his release. The state provided for drug counseling. He was accountable to the parole board, and he submitted to a weekly drug screening. It would appear that he was given the best opportunities for recovery. Unfortunately, he relapsed. No one considered the possibility of demons. He fought a good fight. However, his battle would have been far easier had the demonic issue been addressed.

However, the converse of the above situation is also true. An addict sought help at a church that was "big" in the deliverance ministry. This church tended to believe all problems were demonic and could be solved through the expulsion of demons. Unfortunately, this addict received little help.

Demons are a valid problem, but they are by no means the only problem in the life of the addict. Many factors are involved in breaking the bondage to alcohol and drugs. However, responsible attention to the demonic realm is important.

The last area needing attention is an area I will call "life skills." Most addicts are very adept at surviving on the street. They expertly supply their daily habit. However, recovering addicts or alcoholics are not nearly as competent in living life normally. I define this difficulty as the Rip Van Winkle phenomenon. For a person to be a functioning adult requires certain life experiences. Every child, adolescent, and adult passes through various social and developmental stages. As a person passes through these stages, he develops the skills by which he touches and manages his world. His capacity to relate healthily with others starts at birth and continues to develop with experience. However, if an individual has spent his life anesthetized, life's experiences pass him by in a drug- or alcohol-induced fog. Consequently, if he emerges from addiction, he is usually immature and ill equipped to function adequately in his new drug-free world.

Leigh was just such a person. I saw her for the first time shortly after she detoxed. She began drinking and doing drugs at thirteen, and for the next fourteen years, she did not spend one day sober or straight. Now, at age twenty-seven she was battling to stay clean. Since self-discipline was all but non-existent, she had difficulty keeping a job. Her mind was slow and dull as it tried to recover normal functioning. A relapse appeared unavoidable. She couldn't operate in the world she encountered.

Because Leigh had anesthetized herself for fourteen years, she surfaced from her drug and alcohol stupor at twenty-seven years old chronologically, but emotionally and socially, she had not progressed much past thirteen. Like Rip Van Winkle, she awakened to a different world, one which she was mentally, emotionally, and socially unable to manage. We placed her in a Christian live-in facility for women, where she learned a profession. This ministry also taught her how to grocery shop, to balance a checkbook, and to be an effective parent. She learned how to fill out an employment application and how to interview for a job. The average person takes these skills for granted, but to an individual who is emotionally, mentally, and developmentally immature, they are overpowering obstacles.

Another similar situation involved two heroin addicts who were married to each other. They opted to detox from heroin at the same time. The first time I saw them, they fought like two children. I resisted the urge to put them both in the corner until they could behave. However, what they were experiencing was quite common. Their marital relationship had been built on a drug lifestyle. They emerged relationally and emotionally immature and had to grow up and learn how to relate as adults. This process takes time, experience, and support.

Several years ago, while working at a methadone clinic, I read statistics that estimated that fewer than 4% of heroin addicts fully recover. Though recovery for the general drug and alcohol population might be somewhat better, I was not impressed with the success rate I observed. It seemed that for all of the time, money, and support lavished on the addicts, more success should be expected. While considering these questions, I began visiting a large church in a metropolitan area. One Sunday the pastor asked everyone whom Jesus had set free from drug or alcohol addiction to stand. It would be difficult to estimate how many people stood that day, but I would guess the number went into the hundreds. I was impressed. It appeared to me that the world spends millions of dollars achieving what Jesus accomplished on the cross that is freely available to all who will accept Him.

Alcoholics Anonymous, one of the more successful recovery programs in the world today, gives attention to a "higher power." They recognize the need for supernatural intervention in the life of a recovering addict. However, the only "higher power" that comes "to set the captives free" is Jesus, and whoever Jesus "...sets free is free indeed." Jesus died to save us from not just an eternal hell, but also a hell on earth. Isaiah 61:1-3 says,

> *Jesus died to save us from not just an eternal hell, but also a hell on earth.*

> *"The Spirit of the Lord God is upon Me, because the Lord has anointed Me to preach good tidings to the poor; He has sent Me to heal the brokenhearted, to proclaim liberty to the captives, and the opening of the prison to those who are bound; to proclaim the acceptable year of the Lord, and the day of vengeance of our God: to comfort all who mourn, to console those who mourn in Zion, to give them beauty for ashes, the oil of joy for mourning, the garment of praise for the spirit of heaviness; that they may be called trees of righteousness, the planting of the Lord, that He may be glorified"* (NKJV).

When an addict accepts Jesus as his personal Savior, his heart will change; his goals will change; his lifestyle will change; his thought-life will change. No longer will he be physically and emotionally driven by an addiction. For the addict who is brokenhearted, who is bound and in prison which is mourning, Jesus can and will give beauty for ashes and joy for mourning. Jesus is the Healer and the Deliverer. True freedom will be found only in Him. As you resolve in your heart to give your life to God and to address the necessary issues with His help and direction, freedom will be the result.

The Fortress of Your Freedom

Understanding How to Maintain Freedom Forever

The Fortress of a Daily Walk with Christ

Chapter 18 Jimmy Evans

The past three sections of this book were designed to give you some tools to help you understand what negatively ties you to your past and to set you free from those bondages. This section is designed to help you maintain that freedom. These four chapters will give you insight into four important disciplines of life that insure freedom and blessing. These "fortresses" provide the atmosphere of peace and safety you need in order to receive and retain the ministry of God in your life.

The first and most important element to establishing and maintaining freedom is one's personal relationship with Christ. I have never known a person who received or maintained freedom without it. My wife, Karen, and I can both attest to the power of a daily walk with Christ and how it transforms, energizes, and heals.

Besides Jesus, the most victorious and liberated people who ever lived were Adam and Eve. The Bible says that before the fall, they lived in paradise, where there was no sickness, poverty, or crime. The most important element of their blessedness, though, was the presence of God. According to Genesis, God walked with Adam and Eve in the cool of the day. As long as He was with them, they lived in freedom and perfect harmony.

Bondage for the entire human race began when Adam and Eve rejected God by eating of the fruit of the Tree of the Knowledge of Good and Evil. God had forbidden them to eat of it. When the serpent seduced them to rebel against God for the sake of their own personal benefit, they rejected the One who had created them free and obeyed the one who only sought to destroy them and make a mockery of God's plan for their lives.

Even after Adam and Eve fell, God still loved them and had a plan to restore mankind into a relationship with Him. God's plan was to send His Son, Jesus, to die for their sins and for all the sins of the world. In doing this, Jesus would satisfy the penalty of death that God established for sin and make a way for our relationship with God to be restored.

The theme of the Bible is God's desire to be in good relationship with man. Our relationship with Him is the key of our success and happiness in life. Because we were designed to function in His presence and with His guidance, we won't find complete fulfillment anywhere else.

Our relationship with Jesus begins as we receive Him as the Lord of our life and His death as the payment for our sins. Romans 10:9 says, *"That if thou shalt confess with thy mouth the Lord Jesus, and shalt believe in thine heart that God hath raised him from the dead, thou shalt be saved"* (KJV). Salvation takes place when we submit ourselves to the Lordship of Christ and believe He is the only begotten Son of God who was sent to redeem us.

This salvation is by grace. In other words, it isn't based on how good we are or who we are. It is based on the death and resurrection of Christ. He fulfilled God's requirement for righteousness. Though we are sinful and don't deserve it, Jesus extends perfect righteousness to every person who will put faith in Him and receive His death as the payment for his sins. This is why this story is called the "Gospel"—it is very good news!

In spite of our imperfections and sins, God is in love with us. When we confess our sins and receive Christ Jesus as Lord, our relationship begins. Here is what Ephesians 2:8-9 says about salvation: *"For by grace are ye saved through faith; and that not of yourselves: it is the gift of God: Not of works, lest any man should boast"* (KJV).

God's free gift to us is salvation through Jesus Christ. We don't have to wait until we have "everything together" before we come to Him. In fact, we can't get it together without Him. If you haven't already done so, accept God's gift of forgiveness and eternal life through Jesus Christ right now. Once you invite Christ into your life by faith, He will come in and will live with you forever.

Once we have received Jesus into our hearts, there are three important disciplines we need to establish in our lives. These disciplines will keep our relationship with Christ real, fresh, and growing. They are praying, reading the Bible, and yielding to the Holy Spirit.

Praying

Prayer is one of the greatest privileges we have in this life. The God who created the universe invites us to talk with Him as often as we like about anything we need. Not only does He invite us to come before Him in prayer, but He also promises to hear and answer our prayers if we come by faith.

When I first became a Christian, I learned how to have a daily "quiet time." This was a time in the day that was set apart to spend with the Lord. Though making time for God was challenging at first, I established the discipline of taking the very first of every day to pray and read my Bible. More than thirty years later I still do this, and it has been the backbone of my spiritual growth and relationship with Christ.

I can't explain everything that happens in my prayer times with the Lord, but I can say without a doubt that they are powerful. In my prayer times over the years, God has healed me, spoken to my mind and heart, given me comfort and direction, and granted answers to thousands of prayer requests. Without these quiet times, my life would be totally different today.

I can tell you, as you seek to establish a regular prayer time, that the devil will resist you and try to discourage you. If he can't do that, he'll try to make you so busy that he can crowd God out of your schedule. Resist him with everything in you and never give up. Even if he wins a battle or two, you can still win the war. Make a commitment to take your needs to God in prayer every day. Establish a time and a place to do this. Then fight everything that tries to keep you from it.

In encouraging you to pray, I realize that you may have never been taught how to pray. Over the years I have read many books on the importance and purpose of prayer. I would encourage you to go to your local church or Christian bookstore and ask them to direct you to some good books on prayer. I try to read books on prayer regularly so I can be encouraged and educated as well as having my faith uplifted.

Reading the Bible

Bible reading is another critical foundation in establishing and maintaining a daily walk with Christ. The Bible is unlike any other book. We read many books—the Bible reads us. According to Hebrews 4:12, the Word of God is alive and active. When we read the Scriptures, they begin to heal us, enlighten us, and empower us.

I encourage you to buy a translation of the Bible you can understand. There is nothing spiritual about reading a Bible that doesn't make sense to you. It is also important to find some method of reading through the Bible that feeds your spirit every day, without becoming overwhelming timewise.

I read one chapter in the New Testament, two chapters in the Old Testament, and one chapter in either the Psalms or Proverbs every day. In doing that, I read through the Bible once every year. I have done this for many years. Even though I study the Bible extensively outside of my quiet times, these times in the morning are designed to feed my spirit and put me in communion with the Lord. Again, I can't begin to say how much my Bible reading times mean to me. They are life to me. If I go one or two days without them, I can tell a difference.

3. Yielding to the Holy Spirit

Here is what Jesus said concerning the ministry of the Holy Spirit:

> "Nevertheless I tell you the truth; it is expedient for you that I go away: for if I go not away, the

Even though I study the Bible extensively outside of my quiet times, these times in the morning are designed to feed my spirit and put me in communion with the Lord.

Comforter will not come unto you; but if I depart, I will send him unto you. And when he is come, he will reprove the world of sin, and of righteousness, and of judgment: Of sin, because they believe not on me; of righteousness, because I go to my Father, and ye see me no more; of judgment, because the prince of this world is judged. I have yet many things to say unto you, but ye cannot bear them now. Howbeit when he, the Spirit of truth, is come, he will guide you into all truth: for he shall not speak of himself but whatsoever he shall hear, that shall he speak: and he will shew you things to come. He shall glorify me: for he shall receive of mine, and shall shew it unto you. All things that the Father hath are mine: therefore said I that he shall take of mine, and shall shew it unto you" (John 16:7-15, KJV).

The Holy Spirit has been sent by God to give us power (Acts 1:8), to fill us with the character of Christ (Galatians 5:22), to give us gifts for ministry (1 Corinthians 12), to comfort us (John 16:7), and to lead us into all truth and a closer relationship with Jesus. The ministry of the Holy Spirit is critical to our lives. As we ask God to fill us with His Spirit every day, He will. After asking the Holy Spirit to fill us, we then yield to Him moment by moment as we face the issues of our lives. There is no issue that He is unprepared for or won't help us confront and overcome. Also, as we yield to the Holy Spirit, He will give us understanding into the Scriptures as He also puts our spirits in communion with Christ.

Begin today to commit yourself to building your personal relationship with the Lord. You will find an incredible joy and strength available to you, as you grow closer to the Lord. Your relationship with Christ is the secret of becoming and remaining free.

The Fortress of a Transformed Mind

Chapter 19 Jimmy Evans

"And do not be conformed to this world, but be transformed by the renewing of your mind, that you may prove what is that good and acceptable and perfect will of God" **Romans 12:2 (NKJV).**

The previous chapter stressed the importance of reading the Bible daily because it is essential in building our relationship with Christ. This chapter takes Scripture reading one step further. Not only is the written Word of God important in our relationship with Jesus, but it is also powerful in renewing our minds.

The most powerful cord that ties most of us to our past is the way we think. Lack of truth, ignorance, worldly information, and deception all keep us from the freedom Jesus offers. As Jesus said in John 8:31-32, *"If ye continue in my word, then are ye my disciples indeed; and ye shall know the truth, and the truth shall make you free"* (KJV). This liberating truth offers us freedom in our marriages, families, finances, relationships, ministries, our past, and future. The more we allow it to transform our minds, the more freedom we receive and are able to maintain.

The opposite of this principle is also true. If we have had an encounter with God that produced a healing or deliverance in our lives, the permanence and furtherance of that freedom is found in the continuing ministry of God's Word in our lives. Time and time again, I have seen people receive true ministry and freedom, only to find that after a period of months or years they were back into the same problem again. They always have the same thing in common—healing was the end of their search for God and not the beginning. Those people who have received ministry from the Lord and retained it are those who have entered into a genuine discipleship as a result of their freedom and have allowed God's Word to find a permanent, active place in their lives, renewing and transforming their minds.

As discussed in the last chapter, the first important discipline we need to establish in order to have our minds transformed is a time of daily reading of Scripture. It is my personal conviction that an early morning time is best. The reason for this is that by receiving God's Word into our minds in the morning, it prepares us for the rest of the day. If a person prefers a later time of the day or evening, that is still fine. The importance is not when we read, but that we establish a set time and place to do it, and it becomes a set discipline.

Make sure you find a Bible translation you can understand and choose a reading program that gives you enough to read daily without being too much. I found out a long time ago that the issue of Bible reading isn't how much I can read in one sitting; it is how much sinks into my heart and becomes a part of my life. As you ask the Holy Spirit to guide you through the Scriptures and give you understanding, read it daily and let God's Word sink into your mind.

Once you have begun the process of daily Bible reading, you are then ready to begin a life-changing discipline called biblical meditation. Look at the incredible promise made in the first Psalm to the person who meditates on the Word of God:

> *"Blessed is the man who walks not in the counsel of the ungodly, nor stands in the path of sinners, nor sits in the seat of the scornful; but his delight is in the law of the LORD, and <u>in His law he meditates day and night</u>. He shall be like a tree planted by the rivers of water, that brings forth its fruit in its season, whose leaf also shall not wither; and <u>whatever he does shall prosper</u>.*
>
> *The ungodly are not so, but are like the chaff which the wind drives away. Therefore the ungodly shall not stand in the judgment, nor sinners in the congregation of the righteous. For the LORD knows the way of the righteous, but the way of the ungodly shall perish"* (Psalm 1:1-6, NKJV) [underlines added].

You can purchase all of the success manuals in the world, but the greatest promise any person has for success is through meditation on God's Word. The word *meditate* in Psalms literally means to *ruminate*. It's the same process as when a cow or sheep continues to chew its cud over and over. A

> *You can purchase all of the success manuals in the world, but the greatest promise any person has for success is through meditation on God's Word.*

sheep has five stomachs. As it "ruminates," it continues to swallow and regurgitate its food until the food has become very refined and ready for digestion.

The process of meditation in our lives begins as we read God's Word daily. This begins our feeding. As we read a Scripture verse or story, we then begin to think about it through the day. Probably ninety percent of everything I know about the Bible I learned this way. It is powerful. As I go through my day, I think about something in the Bible that doesn't make sense or something I want to understand more fully. As I meditate, the Holy Spirit begins to show me what this verse means. Meditation also benefits me when I find a Scripture that is relevant to a specific problem or situation and meditate throughout the day on that Scripture.

The process of meditation is transforming. As you continue to digest and regurgitate God's Word throughout the day, you will experience some of the incredible benefits:

- The Word of God becomes revelation knowledge to you. No longer is the Bible dull and lifeless, but it comes alive in your heart and mind.
- Your thinking changes, and your mind is renewed. Hebrews 4:12 says this: *"For the word of God is quick, and powerful, and sharper than any two-edged sword, piercing even to the dividing asunder of soul and spirit, and of the joints and marrow, and is a discerner of the thoughts and intents of the heart"* (KJV).
- When you allow God's Word inside of you, it is alive and begins a healing, enemy-slaying, transforming work.
- Worry, stress, fear, and anxiety are defeated in your life. One of the things I've noticed about the difference when I meditate is a presence of peace that passes understanding. Without meditation on God's Word, one's

mind becomes an open target for unhealthy and unclean thoughts. These thoughts are the fountainhead of worry, fear, and sin. Meditation, on the other hand, fills one's mind with thoughts that are *"of good report, virtuous, and praiseworthy"* (Philippians 4:8).

- Sinful thoughts are defeated. For men battling with lust, biblical meditation is the most powerful and effective means for overcoming it. This is true for any other sin pattern in life. As we allow God's Word to have an abiding place in our minds, the Word defeats the enemies of God and endows us with the power we need to overcome sin. This is a powerful truth.

One more item I want to point out regarding meditation. When you begin to think about the practical side of meditating on God's Word, you're going to wonder how to fulfill all of your other responsibilities and to meditate as well. This is a valid concern. The answer is found in the book of Deuteronomy. When Moses commanded parents to teach their children God's commandments, here is what He said: *"And these words which I command you today shall be in your heart. You shall teach them diligently to your children, and shall talk of them when you sit in your house, when you walk by the way, when you lie down, and when you rise up"* (Deuteronomy 6:6-7, NKJV) [underline added].

According to this Scripture, there are four times Moses commanded parents to teach their children: as they sat around their house; when they were on their way somewhere; when they went to bed at night; and when they woke up in the morning. These times are all natural times to meditate on God's Word. They are also four of the times when sinful and anxious thoughts most attack our minds. If we aren't meditating on God's Word during those times, we will be meditating on something less edifying.

In summary, our minds are the keys to living in freedom. If we are abiding in God's Word, then we will be receiving truth, and that truth will constantly minister freedom and blessing to us. Abiding in God's Word begins as we establish a daily time and place to read God's Word. As we read each day, always asking the Holy Spirit to reveal God's Word to our minds and hearts, that Word begins to sink in and becomes life to us.

Beyond our reading time, we retain in our minds a verse, passage, or Bible story to think about the rest of the day. As we sit around our houses, ride in our cars, and lie on our beds, we "regurgitate" the Scriptures we read earlier. The more we do this during our day, the more refined and powerful the Word of God becomes to us. The process of meditation defeats our mental enemies, restores our souls, and transforms our thinking. The end result is success in every area of life.

Begin today to meditate on God's Word. Every person can do it, whether you have been saved for twenty years or two days. The Holy Spirit is waiting to take you on an incredible journey into the Word of God. Fasten your seat belts! You're about to be transformed!

> *"This Book of the Law shall not depart from your mouth, but you shall meditate in it day and night, that you may observe to do according to all that is written in it. For then you will make your way prosperous, and then you will have good success." Joshua 1:8 (NKJV)*

The Fortress of Accountability

Chapter 20 Jimmy Evans

"And let us consider one another in order to stir up love and good works, not forsaking the assembling of ourselves together, as is the manner of some, but exhorting one another, and so much the more as you see the Day approaching" **Hebrews 10:24-25 (NKJV).**

Support groups are becoming very popular around the country today. The reason is that they work. Pastors, psychologists, and therapists are all discovering that people get more help, get it quicker, and retain it longer when they are involved in a support group.

Personally, I would not be where I am today apart from Jesus and His wonderful grace and love towards me. He saved and transformed me, impacting my life like no other. However, second to Jesus' influence is the relationship He established with my brothers and sisters in Christ. I wouldn't be here today if they had not stayed with me during hard times and kept me

> *Without a doubt,
> those who go the
> farthest in their walk
> with Christ are those
> who are committed to
> Christian fellowship
> and who are
> accountable to other
> Christians.*

accountable during weak times. The Church—the Body of Christ—is a beautiful and powerful family that all of us need. In spite of all of its imperfections, the Church is God's only physical instrument on this earth. Even though God can do much without the Church, He chooses not to. Therefore, committed participation with a local body of believers is an essential part of receiving ministry, maturing in Christ, and growing in our own ministry.

As a pastor of an eight-thousand-member church, I have an opportunity to observe the lives of many people. Without a doubt, those who go the farthest in their walk with Christ are those who are committed to Christian fellowship and who are accountable to other Christians. Though I don't believe that the Bible teaches that we are to dominate and control each other spiritually or to breach the sovereignty of a person's home life and personal privacy, I do believe in voluntary accountability.

When we become a committed part of a local fellowship, the next step is to make ourselves visible and accountable to the leadership and other members in the church. Obviously, for any of us to feel comfortable doing that, we need to diligently pray and seek out a healthy, Bible-believing church. The perfect church does not exist, but we can find a healthy one where the Word of God is preached. Once we find a church to which we believe the Lord has led us, we need to do more than just attend. We need to become an active, accountable part. This means that we come out of our comfort zone and allow other people to know us intimately and help us to mature in Christ. Through teaching, sharing, ministry, fellowship, and worship, we receive God's manifold ministry that He has ordained and anointed to flow through His body—the Church.

Unfortunately, there are many people who constantly find fault with the Church and other Christians. They believe this fault justifies staying aloof from fellowship and accountability. Regardless of their arguments, I have not found one single person in the past 30+ years of walking with Christ who alienated himself from committed Christian fellowship, and who continued to mature spiritually or did anything great for God.

Look around at the people who are mature in Christ and have remained faithful to the Lord for many years. They are people who are accountable and involved in healthy fellowship. Conversely, if you will examine the lives of those who gave up, backslid, or never matured, they were either involved in unhealthy fellowship or none at all. The issue of Christian fellowship and accountability is critical.

When a wolf wants to find a sheep to eat, he doesn't attack the middle of a flock or a sheep close to the shepherd. He looks for a straggler. If he can find an independent sheep, separated from the flock, he can have an easy meal. Regardless of our excuses, when we remain separated from close Christian fellowship, we are in spiritual danger. We live in a spiritually severe and dangerous world. The power of sin has never been greater. Spiritual success demands that we humble ourselves and admit that we need the safety, support, and ministry of fellow believers.

When I first began going to church, I felt uncomfortable. Having just been saved, I was unfamiliar with the people and the processes of church. I immediately saw problems in the people and the system, and I knew I had a choice to make. I could either let my feelings and the problems I saw give me a reason to avoid relationship or leave the church altogether, or I could commit my life to making the church system and people better. I chose the latter.

I have been hurt and disappointed in church life and by Christians, but I have also been blessed in extraordinary ways by both. A church family parallels a real family. Not everyone is perfect, but it is God's place for us to belong and mature. If you haven't already done so, make a decision right now to become a committed, accountable, and constructive part of a local church.

When you become a part of a church, find a Sunday school class or Bible study group where you can meet people and develop closer relationships. God will use these relationships to bless you and keep you accountable. He will also use you to bless others. Never would I have received the healing and ministry necessary to set me free, nor would I have discovered the ministry I have today if it hadn't been for my dear friends in the Church.

Regardless of where you are or what your experiences have been in the past, do whatever it takes to become committed and accountable. You will find the Church and fellow believers to be a fortress of love, prayer, and support to help you through the struggles in life. God also wants to use your life to be a fortress for others. However, this can't happen at home by yourself or by slipping anonymously in and out of church. You must take a bold step to make yourself a part of the Church community and, regardless of the cost or struggles, stay there! In that place, God will continue and expand His work in your life as you are ministered to and held accountable by your brothers and sisters in Christ.

The Fortress of Spiritual Warfare

Chapter 21 Ann Billington

"Finally, my brethren, be strong in the Lord and in the power of His might. Put on the whole armor of God, that you may be able to stand against the wiles of the devil. For we do not wrestle against flesh and blood, but against principalities, against powers, against the rulers of the darkness of this age, against spiritual hosts of wickedness in the heavenly places. Therefore take up the whole armor of God, that you may be able to withstand in the evil day, and having done all, to stand. Stand therefore, having girded your waist with truth, having put on the breastplate of righteousness, and having shod your feet with the preparation of the gospel of peace; above all taking the shield of faith with which you will be able to quench all the fiery darts of the wicked one. And take the helmet of salvation, and the sword of the Spirit, which is the word of God; praying always with all prayer and supplication in the Spirit, being watchful to this end with all perse-*

verance and supplication for all the saints" Ephesians 6:10-18 (NKJV).

Throughout the epistles, the apostle Paul uses military imagery to describe our lives on earth. Clearly, Christians are engaged in a battle. An explanation of the spiritual warfare surrounding the Christian is clearly presented in Ephesians 6:10-18. Jesus provided for our healing and deliverance through His death and resurrection. However, just because we are healed of our past and set free from demonic influences, doesn't mean the devil disarms himself and surrenders. Paul reiterates that point in Ephesians 6:12. He teaches us that our battle is not against flesh and blood, but against evil powers, principalities, and rulers.

From the time of the Roman Empire to the present, Christians and Christianity have come under attack. History recounts story after story where Christians were forced to flee from one country to another. Even today, we increasingly hear of civil liberty violations against Christians. However, Paul wants all of us to understand that some of the attacks we encounter are not what they seem.

Within the world, there is an evil energy at work, whose goal it is to destroy Christ's kingdom. Rather than hate those who attack us, the Christian should hate the evil in the spiritual realm that sponsors that wickedness. As long as Jesus delays His return to earth, the enemy will make attempts to "steal, kill, and destroy." We, as Christians, must learn how to look beyond the natural to the spirit realm and engage an evil enemy in combat. Unless we understand this truth, it will be difficult for us to retain the ground we've taken in Jesus' name. Paul provides us with instructions in Ephesians chapter 6.

Jesus furnishes armor for us so that we can *"...stand against the wiles of the devil."* According to Strong's Lexicon, "wiles" means "lie in wait, cunning arts, deceit, craft, trickery." The implication of this word is that the enemy lies in wait and uses cunning arts and trickery to deceive us, leading us back into bondage. However, protection is available in Jesus. We are not defenseless, but have armor and weapons at our disposal.

Basically, Paul gives us six pieces of armor and some tactical information with which to engage the enemy. He encourages us to put on the whole armor of God, implying that it is for our protection and our warfare. The first piece of armor mentioned is the girdle, which is a belt. From the belt the Roman soldier hung his sword and attached his breastplate. His major weapon and his major defense were both attached and dependent on the belt.

Paul instructs us to gird ourselves with truth. As the belt was for the Roman soldier, so truth is the belt upon which so much depends. Deception is a chief tool of the enemy and can be produced by sin, pride, an absence of accountability, rebellion, and lies. To stay free, we must sincerely face the truth without denial or dishonesty. To enable us to do that, Jesus furnishes us with a lamp of reality. Hebrews 4:12 says the Word of God is the discerner of the thoughts and intents of the heart.

When we look into the light of the Word, it reveals the unsanctified and unhealed areas in our lives. Unfortunately, many people don't like what they see, and they begin a dance with denial, which produces deception and further bondage. The first piece of armor that must be in place is the belt of truth. Without it the battle is lost before it even begins.

The second piece of armor mentioned by Paul is the breastplate of righteousness. Righteousness is right standing with God. This is a position the Christian doesn't earn, but receives as a free gift of God through Jesus. His death on the cross paid for our sins. Therefore, through acceptance of Christ through faith, we receive the gift of righteousness. Because we are in right standing with God, this breastplate protects our hearts and nature.

The Roman soldier's breastplate protected his most vital organs, which if injured could produce instant death. Our righteousness protects us from the spiritual death, which the enemy so desires to achieve. The breastplate protects us from Satan's deathblows of condemnation and shame before God. Realizing our own failures and sins, we place our confidence in the finished work of Jesus on the cross. Therefore, Satan's attempts to discourage or condemn us are foiled. Without the breastplate of righteousness, we don't stand a chance against Satan. Doing battle with the enemy without this piece of armor is foolish.

When we stand in battle array, the breastplate of righteousness is between the enemy and us. He recognizes the invulnerability of the breastplate and honors this position of the believer in the kingdom of God. Don't let the enemy try to make you stand in your own righteousness. Also, don't allow him to convince you that Jesus' atoning blood wasn't shed for you. In order to access the incredible power of the blood of Christ, we must take our eyes off how good or bad we are and place them on Jesus. As we do this, we must believe by faith that Christ didn't die for righteous people, but for sinners like us. As we accept His performance on the cross as our righteousness, we are then covered by God and, thereby, protected from the enemy.

Once we have put on the breastplate of righteousness, Ephesians 6:15 then exhorts us to have our feet shod *"with the preparation of the gospel of peace."* The word "peace" here in the Greek language has several meanings. It can mean a state of harmony between individuals or peace with God through the blood of Jesus.

The Roman soldier wore sandals with spikes on the soles. These spikes enabled him to better grip the ground; hence there was less chance that he would lose his footing during battle. A soldier who loses his footing during battle is an easy target for a skillful swordsman. Peace in the form of reconciliation was first brought to us through the cross. With the gospel of peace, the Christian learns true love, a commodity that was absent until Jesus' time. If our feet are grounded in love, peace will abound. The enemy wants us to slip and fall, knowing that in losing our footing, we become vulnerable.

When peace is absent, divisiveness and discord are present. Too many churches have lost their footing and are attempting to stand against an enemy who has them pinned to the ground. Peace is gone, and internal warfare is raging. The enemy knows we will fail if we attempt to deliver a gospel of love while our feet are shod with turmoil and discord. To effectively stand against the enemy, we must pursue peace and love.

As the feet are the foundation upon which the physical body stands, so peace and love are the foundational principles upon which the Gospel stands. Romans 12:8 says, *"If it is possible, as much as depends on you, live peaceably with all men"* (NKJV).

As foot soldiers in the kingdom of God, we need to be certain that our feet are shod with the Gospel of peace and not with unforgiveness, hate, and judgment.

> When peace is absent, divisiveness and discord are present.

The fourth piece of armor is the shield of faith. The Roman soldier carried a shield that was constructed of two pieces of wood, which were glued together. The entire outer surface of the shield was covered with leather. It measured four feet tall and two-and-one-half feet wide. Archers dipped the tips of their arrows in a flammable substance, and shot them at their enemy. The flaming arrow penetrated the leather and wood and extinguished itself. Paul tells us that our shield is faith, and with this faith, Satan's flaming arrows will also be extinguished.

Satan's darts take the form of attacks, deceptions, temptations, and accusations. He assaults our minds with every conceivable thought in an attempt to regain lost territory. In order to remain healed, it is important to control our thought-life. The enemy has access to our minds and interjects his thoughts and ideas into them. The twist is that we naturally assume that those thoughts are our creation, when in reality Satan is the author.

James 1:14 says each one is tempted when he is drawn away by his own desires and enticed. The enemy can't make you sin. All he can do is present you with the opportunity to sin. What he needs and wants is your cooperation. Keeping one's shield of faith in place is important for continued freedom. When the enemy presents you with the urge to sin, your faith must rise up to extinguish the thoughts that are endeavoring to root in your mind. The shield of faith intercepts the fiery darts of doubt, discouragement, and defeat peddled by the devil. Faith in Jesus and His continued power and presence in one's life will counter the maneuvers of Satan. One of the main occupations of the devil is to discredit God's promises, power, and presence in one's life. As each of us puts faith in God's character and Word on a daily basis, we uncover and disarm the schemes of our enemy.

The fifth piece of armor Paul discusses is the helmet of salvation. The Roman soldier wore a helmet, which protected his head from mortal injury. Like the breastplate, the helmet protected a strategic organ, the brain, which if injured could cause death. Everything a human does or thinks must originate in the brain. The helmet of salvation protects the Christian's mind. His mind is his command center. For the most part, a person doesn't act unless he thinks first. Therefore, the battle Satan fights largely occurs in one's mind.

Keeping our shield of faith upright and ready for battle is important. However, it is equally important to control our thoughts. Before we knew Jesus, our thought-life was worldly and subject to our senses. However, after we were saved, new data from the Word of God was introduced. This data, even though foreign at first, provides us with the implements of war to regain our minds and with the power to protect them from further intrusion.

To maintain our deliverance and healing, we renew our minds through the Word of God, learning to think thoughts that are consistent with people who walk in the power of the Holy Spirit. With the helmet of salvation firmly in place, little room is given to the enemy for his reattachment. When our minds are filled with light and truth, we walk in safety and peace.

The last weapon is the sword of the Spirit, which is the Word of God. Though the sword was at times used defensively, it was the Roman soldier's only offensive weapon. Every other piece of armor listed in Ephesians 6 was defensive, designed to protect the soldier from harm. However, the sword was the instrument used to pierce the heart of the enemy. When Jesus was led by the Holy Spirit into the wilderness to be tempted, He resisted the temptations of the enemy by using the Word of God. With every temptation hurled at Him by the devil, Jesus responded with, *"It is written."*

When the enemy attacks us in an attempt to deceive, torment, or scare us, like Jesus, we should counter with the Word of God. As Satan honored God's Word in the wilderness, he has to honor the same Word today. God's Word is powerful. Hebrew 4:12 says, *"For the word of God is living and powerful, and sharper than any two-edged sword, piercing even to the division of soul and spirit, and of joints and marrow, and is a discerner of the thoughts and intents of the heart"* (NKJV). The enemy can't stand against the Word of God.

Finally, in Ephesians 6:18 Paul gives us some practical instructions regarding warfare. He says to pray always with all prayer and supplication in the Spirit. Prayer is significant in spiritual warfare. Whether an army is on the move or in position to attack, it doesn't want to lose communication with the generals located behind the lines at field headquarters. A good soldier communicates with his commanders and is unswervingly obedient. The foot soldier hovering in a foxhole knows he doesn't have a clear grasp of the overall battle. He knows little beyond his point of entrenchment and is totally dependent on his leaders to safely and successfully direct him through the battle.

Prayer is a communication link to our General. He understands the battle. He sees the big picture and has wisdom beyond that of the foot soldier. We pray and depend on Him to guide us into a conflict we can't see. Jesus stayed in close communication with field headquarters. When challenged about the miracles He was performing, He stated that He only did what He saw His father doing (John 5:19).

Frequently, Jesus withdrew to lonely places to pray. He didn't operate spontaneously; He was obedient to His General, who gave Him His orders. While battling our unseen enemy, we too must be diligent in our efforts to communicate with God. We are not the Lone Ranger, but a part of an army where communication and obedience are vital. Submitting ourselves to God is essential to preparing for successful warfare against the devil (James 4:7).

Another form of communication with God is praise and worship—an activity that the enemy detests. Not only does praise put the enemy on the run, but it also elevates our spirits, lifts our hearts, and encourages us. In Acts 16:24, Paul and Silas were imprisoned in the Greek city of Macedonia. They were incarcerated because Paul had cast out a spirit of divination from a woman who persistently followed them. As a result of charges brought against them, they were confined under tight security to the innermost part of the prison. *"At midnight Paul and Silas were praying and singing hymns to God, and the prisoners were listening to them"* (Acts 16:25, NKJV).

Suddenly, there was a great earthquake, shaking the foundations of the prison and throwing open the prison doors. Paul and Silas were in prayer and singing hymns prior to their supernatural release. In the process of prayer, don't neglect praise as a tool against the enemy. It focuses our eyes on God, where they need to be, and prepares us to face anything that is coming against us.

Lastly, Paul says to persevere. In a microwave society that is accustomed to fast foods, instant home entertainment, miracle health cures, mobile communications, and supersonic travel, patience and perseverance are not our finest qualities. We want everything to take place immediately. However, when battling spiritual forces, perseverance is one of the most important virtues we can possess. The enemy wants to assault us as he did Job. His plan is to wear us down, as with Job, until we deny God and give up. With God's hand removed from Job, Satan believed Job would fail the test, but Job didn't give in. He stood firm and in the end received back double what he had lost. We also must not give up. Like Job, we need to persevere and outlast the enemy.

James 4:7 says, *"Submit yourselves therefore to God. Resist the devil, and he will flee from you"* (KJV). If we resist the devil long

> Though the enemy does roam the earth like a roaring lion seeking whom he may destroy, God didn't leave us here to battle and struggle without effective weapons.

enough, he will retreat. It is important that we never give ground to the enemy. He will press us until he is convinced that we will not budge in our determination and convictions. Ephesians 6:13 tells us to stand against the evil day. Paul goes on to say that after we have done everything, continue "to stand." In other words, don't succumb to the devil's harassment, and never give up.

Though the enemy does roam the earth like a roaring lion, seeking whom he may destroy, God didn't leave us here to battle and struggle without effective weapons. Rather, He left us powerful tools that not only defeat the enemy, but also keep him at bay once he has been vanquished. Luke 10:19 says, *"Behold, I give you the authority to trample on serpents and scorpions, and over all the power of the enemy, and nothing shall by any means hurt you"* (NKJV). Using the authority of Jesus Christ, we need to bear our armor, take up our shield and sword, and prepare for battle. Jesus has given us the victory!

About
the Author

Jimmy Evans

Jimmy Evans is one of America's leading authorities on family and marriage relationships. He is founder and president of MarriageToday™, an international marriage ministry which began in 1994. *MarriageToday with Jimmy and Karen* broadcasts to more than 80 million homes across America each week as well as to more than 200 countries worldwide. Jimmy and Karen are passionate about the cause of marriage and have devoted themselves to encouraging and training couples in how to build strong and fulfilling marriages and families.

Through television, the Internet, seminars, DVDs, CDs, books and other printed publications, Jimmy shares practical, biblical truths to equip couples for success. Jimmy has authored many books and created over one hundred resource materials to help build and strengthen relationships. Some of his best-known works are *Marriage on the Rock, Our Secret Paradise, The Stress-Free Marriage* and his most recent book, *The Fig Leaf Conspiracy.* Jimmy is a popular church and conference speaker, teaching marriage seminars across the country. Jimmy and Karen have been married for more than 35 years and have two married children and three grandchildren.

Discover MarriageToday

MarriageToday, founded by Jimmy and Karen Evans, is called to establish, strengthen, save and restore family and marriage relationships through a biblical message of healing, restoration, hope and encouragement.

We are committed to providing families with the teaching and tools they need to succeed through our TV broadcast, literature, resources, seminars and the Internet. And dedicated people are joining with us in our mission through prayer and giving. We are changing the future of our nation—one home at a time.

Find out more about MarriageToday at www.marriagetoday.com.

MarriageToday Resources

Dream Marriage

This monthly DVD & CD with study guides is the result of Jimmy and Karen Evans' passion for, and decades of experience in, helping couples just like you. And it is unlike anything else available today.

Go to **OurDreamMarriage.com** to see streaming video samples and to learn more about what it means to be among a special group of couples that are building lasting, joy-filled marriages—for themselves and for others.

Find out more at ourdreammarriage.com.

Marriage on the Rock

In an age of disposable marriage and information overload, where can couples turn for real answers that will make their relationships work? Only to God. **Marriage on the Rock** clearly details God's principles that will turn disillusioned, divorce-bound marriages into satisfying dream relationships.

Available as:

Curriculum Kit | Discussion Guide | Workbook | Paperback Book | DVD Series | CD Series

Curriculum kit includes DVDs, paperback book, leader's guide, couple's guide, group discussion guide, & more.

Sex, Love & Communication

Would you believe someone who told you that God's plan for marriage includes fulfilling sex, romantic love, and healthy, vibrant communication? You should, because it's true!

In **Sex, Love & Communication**, Jimmy Evans explains important truths that will help you create a beautiful, passionate marriage other couples will want to imitate.

Available as:
CD Series | DVD Series

Our Secret Paradise

In **Our Secret Paradise**, couples can discover the healing journey of marriage that begins when two people say "I do." Through practical discussions and humorous illustrations of the ups and downs of marriage, relationship expert Jimmy Evans takes readers on a journey of discovery toward the keys to a strong and beautiful marriage relationship.

Available as:
Hardback Book | CD Series | DVD Series

Every Great Marriage

The greatest marriages on earth have some simple but powerful things in common. They are the insights, viewpoints, habits and techniques that cause relationships to flourish. You can put these elements to work in your relationship.

Available in:
CD Series | DVD Series

The Mountaintop of Marriage

It's a powerful resource, which guides you step-by-step on a journey of revelation and vision for your family.

Available as:
Vision Retreat Workbook

To order these or other marriage-enriching resources, call **1-800-380-6330** or visit **marriagetoday.com**

One Devotional

You can rediscover the joy of your relationship by making your marriage a top priority, and that's what the **One Devotional** is about. This 52-week devotional book provides basic principles for building the marriage of your dreams, plus thought-provoking discussion starters and fun activities to complete together.

For more information, visit onedevotional.com.

Available as:
Hardback Book

7 Secrets of Successful Families

Among other things **7 Secrets of Successful Families** reveals: how to communicate sensitive family issues and resolve conflicts; how a healthy balance of affection and accountability creates stability and harmony; how to establish and maintain correct priorities that keep your family on course for success; and how your home life can become pleasant and secure.

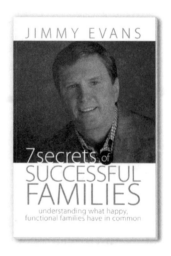

Available as:
Paperback Book | CD Series

Jimmy Evans & Ann Billington **Freedom From Your Past**

The Keys to Sexual Fulfillment

From creation, God intended married couples to enjoy sex. Yet today, as the entertainment industry distorts sexuality, God's intentions are misunderstood. As a result, many married couples experience frustration, and hurt, instead of finding the tremendous pleasure and fulfillment designed by God for marriage.

Available as:
Mini-Book

A Mind Set Free

In a time when the media is screaming "sexuality and sensitivity," here's a book that will help you stay focused and free of sexual temptation. Discover five critical areas to guard in your life, for pillars of moral integrity, and how biblical meditation can help you stay clear of temptation.

Available as:
Mini-Book

The Indestructible Marriage

Have you ever tried to open something that seemed impossible? The packaging was so securely wrapped that no matter what tool you used, it was impenetrable? Our marriages should be the same. We need to be cautious to keep our relationships safe and alert to any danger signs. You and your spouse have the ability to safeguard your relationship and build within it a place of joy, intimacy, security, pleasure and permanence.

Available as:
CD Series | DVD Series